the kingdom of the cat

Roni Jay

the kingdom of the cat

Roni Jay

FIREFLY BOOKS

A FIREFLY BOOK

Copyright © 2000 Quintet Publishing Limited

First Printing

U.S. Cataloging-in-Publication Data
Jay, Roni.
        The kingdom of the cat/Roni Jay.
[224] p. : col ill. : cm. (maps)
Includes bibliographical references and index.
Summary : A history of cat's relationship with
humans; its domestication, and role in art, legend,
myth, and literature throughout history.
ISBN 1-55209-491-X (bound)
ISBN 1-55209-480-4 (pbk.)
1. Cats. 2. Cats – Miscellanea. 3. Cats – Anecdotes.
I. Title.
636.8 –dc21   2000   CIP

Canadian Cataloguing in Publication Data
Jay, Roni.
        The kingdom of the cat/Roni Jay.
Includes bibliographical references and index.
ISBN 1-55209-491-X (bound)
ISBN 1-55209-480-4 (pbk)
1. Cats. I. Title.

SP442.J39 2000   636.8   c99-932890-5

Published in Canada in 2000 by
Firefly Books Ltd.
3680 Victoria Park Avenue
Willowdale, Ontario
M2H 3K1

Published in the United States in 2000 by
Firefly Books (U.S.) Inc.
P.O. Box 1338, Ellicot Station
Buffalo, New York
14205

Book code: TBC

This book was conceived, designed, and produced by Quintet Publishing Limited
6 Blundell Street, London N7 9BH

Editors: Sally Green, Amanda Leung, Carine Tracanelli
Art Directors: Simon Daley, Sharanjit Dhol
Designer: Steve West

Creative Director: Richard Dewing
Publisher: Oliver Salzmann

Jacket Picture Credits
Front cover: Superstock Limited
Back cover, top: Patrick Cone Photography
Back cover, top left: E. T. Archive
Back cover, bottom: Roger Tabor

Typeset in Great Britain by Central Southern Typesetters, Eastbourne
Manufactured in Hong Kong by Regent Publishing Services Limited
Printed in Singapore by Star Standard Industries (Pte) Limited

Contents

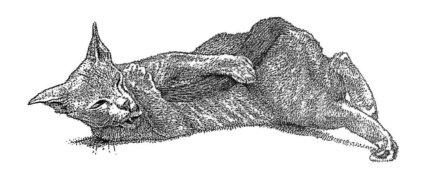

Introduction

Cats are among the most versatile of creatures on earth, and wild cats have spread across the globe to almost every continent. From the North American lynx through the Scottish wild cat, the African lion through the jaguar of South America, cats have populated scrubland and rainforests, deserts, and snowcapped mountains.

But perhaps the cat's greatest achievement has been to inhabit our own homes. Cats were first domesticated in Egypt about four thousand years ago, because they proved invaluable for protecting the grain stores from rats and mice. From there, the domestic cat expanded its territory through the Mediterranean and up into Northern Europe with the Romans, and in the opposite direction, through Asia as far as China and Japan. Cats helped keep the rat population under control on trading ships and so wherever Europeans traveled, they took their cats with them. You now find domestic cats all around the world.

But the story of the cat's relationship with humans is far from simple. Cats have always had a divine or supernatural quality for humans; it wasn't long after their domestication that the Egyptians began to regard them as sacred, and they became associated with some of the most important gods of the Nile region. This association carried over to the gods of classical Greece and Rome, and from there to the Scandinavian gods. But as Christianity gained credence, so these gods were reviled, and their symbolic companions along with them. At the same time, the cats of the East were still enjoying sacred status. The temple cats of the Buddhists were highly revered as guardians of the temples, and it was thought that people's souls transmigrated into cats when they died.

above: **Sketches by Kay Gallwey.**

left: **A hungry cat begging for food, mid-nineteenth century. The cat's fortunes have fluctuated throughout history.**

For centuries, the cats of the West were regarded with suspicion at the very least, and were the subject of many superstitions which still linger to the present day. Anyone who comments on the bad luck bestowed by a black cat crossing their path, or who believes that a cat should not be left alone with a sleeping baby in case it suffocates it, is echoing ancient beliefs connecting cats with the devil.

But the cat has slowly made a comeback in the West, and now vies with the dog for the position of humans' favorite pet. If you are not overrun with rats and mice, a cat has no real practical purpose. But the cat somehow commands love and respect – as any cat owner knows – and merely to have a cat with you is reward enough for many.

The Kingdom of the Cat tells the story of the cat and its roller-coaster history, explaining its place in myth and legend, witchcraft, art and literature, and the development of new breeds of cat. (Surely the greatest flattery we can pay to any animal is to create dozens of new varieties of it.)

It was the cat's air of mystery and independence which earned it its early reputation as a creature to be worshipped, and the same inscrutability which made it such an easy target for the religious zealots of the Middle Ages. But the wheel has come full circle and today we once again regard cats with the respect and awe which they commanded when they were first domesticated.

right: **Sleeping kitten posing with a miniature crown. Cats now command affection and respect.**

above: **African wildcats, members of the *felis* genus, are direct ancestors of the domestic cat.**

the origins
of the
domestic
cat

Early evolution

The first primitive mammals to appear on earth evolved about 200 million years ago; all of today's mammals have evolved from these first warm-blooded creatures that were covered in fur or hair, and that suckled their young.

above: **All members of the cat family are carnivorous, eating a diet made up exclusively of vertebrates.**

However, these animals were small, and had no opportunity to dominate because the Earth already had a dominant group of animals: the dinosaurs.

About 70 million years ago the dinosaurs disappeared, for reasons which are still uncertain. But regardless of what it was that did for the dinosaurs, it gave the mammals a huge boost; especially the group of mammals known as the carnivores—the meat-eaters. There are now two chief groups of carnivores: the dog-like carnivores which include animals such as wolves, bears, pandas (which were originally carnivorous), weasels, badgers, and otters; and the cat-like carnivores, which we'll look at in more detail later on. Many carnivores eat a mixed diet, and today almost the only carnivores which eat a diet made up exclusively of vertebrates are the cats.

above: **The skull of a saber-tooth tiger, best known of the now extinct early felids.**

above: **The mongoose is another unlikely relative, yet its behavior is very similar to that of cats.**

below: **Spotted hyena cub in the Masai Mara, Kenya. Cats are closely related to this doglike animal.**

The earliest carnivores

Different groups of carnivores evolved alongside each other, and the most successful group evolved into the carnivores which inhabit the Earth now—the miacids. The first of these were forest-dwellers and they looked something like martens. They are thought to have had retracting claws, an athletic body, and specialized teeth for cutting and tearing meat, which made them ideally suited to climbing trees and hunting.

The miacids' other great advantage was that they had a larger brain than the other carnivores around at the time; an advantage sufficient to give them the edge over the other carnivores, which eventually became extinct, while the miacids went on to rule the Earth for millions of years. In fact, until the rise of humans, the descendents of the miacids were at the top of the food chain all over the globe.

The cat emerges

In time, the miacids gave rise to several new groups of carnivores. Among these were the canids (dogs), and the viverrids (civets, genets, and mongooses). The civets in the second group were responsible for yet another creature, known as *Pseudoailurus* (which means "false cat"). This was almost a cat, since it had the teeth of a true cat and almost walked on the tips of its toes, as all cats do. This animal appeared about 25 million years ago. The final stage in the process of evolving the cat was completed about 12 million years ago, when the first true cats appeared; descendants of *Pseudoailurus*. These were the first creatures of the group known as Felidae—the cats. Most of the early felids have long since become extinct (the saber-tooth tiger being the best known) but many have evolved further into the cats—both wild and domestic—which still survive and thrive. The cats are now the only widespread group of true carnivores left on earth, still eating an almost exclusively meat diet.

The cat's relatives

The cat family originally evolved from a group of carnivores known as the verrids. This group also includes mongooses, genets, hyenas, and civets, making these the cat family's closest relatives. All these groups of animals share certain common features, the most distinctive being the structure of their skulls. All of them have short, powerful jaws, superbly evolved for biting, and almost all are highly developed and skilled predators.

It can come as a surprise to learn that cats are closely related to the ferretlike mongoose, or the doglike hyena. But if you look beyond the outside appearance of these animals to their behavior and the way they function as predators, the similarities become obvious. The mongoose and the hyena are both almost exclusively carnivorous, and can crunch through thick bones with their strong jaws. Unlike cats, however, hyenas will feed on carrion as well as on fresh prey they hunt down for themselves.

Civets and genets

The closest relative of all to the cats is the civet; it was the civet family from which cats originally evolved. Civets, sometimes known as civet cats, look very like cats. They have the same shaped heads and bodies as cats, though their tails are longer in proportion to the size of their bodies. Civets are forest-dwelling animals, and, unlike the cat family, they eat fruit and invertebrates as well as the small mammals and birds on which small cats typically feed.

In the tropical forests of Africa, you can find a relative of the cat which looks very much like a small cat. The

above: **Genets are not actually cats, but are very closely related.**

right: **Leopard with its kill, a baby waterbuck.**

genet is about the size of a domestic cat, and has a cat-shaped body and head, although the snout is a little longer and the tail longer and bushier than a cat's. It even has spotted markings and a banded tail similar to many cat species including the domestic cat. The genet is nocturnal and lives on insects, birds, and small mammals.

The closest nonrelative

As they evolved, cats populated every continent of the globe apart from two: Antarctica and Australia. The reason for this is continental drift; these two continents broke away from the others before the cat began to evolve. But Australia came up with its own answer to the cat: the marsupial.

These creatures (which all have pouches to carry their young) moved to the top of the food chain, and are highly developed hunters. Some even have sharp cutting teeth just as cats do. In other words, in the absence of any species of cat, nature evolved an alternative to fulfill the same ecological function. Although unrelated to cats, these animals have many similarities to them; there is even one species called the "marsupial cat," so named because it is similar in both looks and behavior.

above: **Marsupials such as koalas are Australia's answer to the cat, fulfilling the same ecological function.**

The cat family

The cat family, *Felidae*, has three branches: *Panthera, Felix,* and *Acinonyx*. The first
of these contains the big cats, and the second includes all the smaller cats. The
third branch, *Acinonyx*, contains only one species, the cheetah.

top left: **The jaguar's range spans an area from southern California down to the pampas of Argentina.**
below: **Lions are one of the few members of the cat family that can roar.**

top right and below: **Small cats such as the Scottish wild cat and the Northern Lynx are among the most successful animal groups, occupying a huge range of habitats.**

Panthera

This branch (or genus) of the cat family contains the larger species of cat: lion, tiger, leopard, snow leopard, clouded leopard, and jaguar. The most obvious feature which sets these cats apart from the rest, other than their greater size, is the fact that they can roar—they are sometimes known as the "roaring cats." They have a bone at the base of the tongue partly made of cartilage, which enables them to roar. Apart from the jaguar of South America and the cougar of North America, all the big cats live in Africa or Asia.

Felix

There is some disagreement over the number of species into which the cat family can be classified, but most zoologists agree that there are just over 30 species of small cats around the world, on every continent apart from Antarctica and Australia, and these are found in the *Felix* branch of the cat family. These include the lynx, the puma, the ocelot, and the wildcats of Europe and Africa. They also include the domestic cat, *Felis catus*.

The small cats have managed to adapt to inhabit virtually every climate, from the freezing temperatures of the Canadian and Scandinavian winters, through the deserts of Africa, and the humid jungles of South America. The *Felis* genus includes, among others, the direct ancestors of the domestic cat, most commonly reckoned to be the jungle cat and the African wildcat, and it is interesting to see the connection between them.

The solitary cheetah

The cheetah has evolved separately from other cats for at least three million years, and is a highly skilled hunter which relies heavily on its speed. As every student knows, the cheetah is the fastest land mammal, and can reach speeds of over 60 miles per hour. Unlike other cats, however, it cannot stalk its prey, and if its attack is not successful during its initial burst of speed, it has little chance of making a kill. It also differs from other members of the cat family in that it cannot retract its claws fully. Cheetahs are solitary animals, so they also lack the opportunity to share in a group kill as lions do, for example.

right: **Despite its size, the cheetah is not classified as a big cat, Among other differences, it can purr continuously but cannot roar as the lion can.**
below: **Cheetahs lie down with their front paws stretched out, like the big cats. Small cats tend to tuck in their paws.**

Wildcats

The nearest relative of the domestic cat, and the one from which it is most directly descended, is the wildcat. The wildcat has an enormous range, stretching from Scotland down to southern Africa, and across Europe into the Middle East. Apart from the domestic cat, this is one of the most extensive ranges of any cat species.

The wildcat's numbers have declined over the centuries as its natural habitats have been destroyed—particularly the forests of Europe—and it has been hunted

below: **The wildcat has the widest distribution of any field (indicated by red areas on map), ranging from northern parts of Europe down to the tip of southern Africa, and eastward through the Middle East into Asia. Within its range, a number of subspecies have been identified, with the African population, from which the domestic cat was originally descended, sometimes being considered a separate species.**

as vermin. Nevertheless it still survives, and thrives in places, having adapted to live in hotter and less forested habitats such as Africa. Wildcats should not be confused with feral cats. A feral cat is a domestic cat which lives and breeds in the wild, fending for itself and its family. A wildcat is a member of a completely different species of the cat family, although a closely related one.

Types of wildcat

Although there is only one species of wildcat, it is divided into several subspecies. The African wildcat, which is the one from which the domestic cat is directly descended, is sometimes considered to be a separate species from other wildcats. The only parts of Africa which the African wildcat has not succeeded in populating are the areas of very dense jungle or extremely arid desert. The African wildcat chiefly eats small mammals, although if hungry

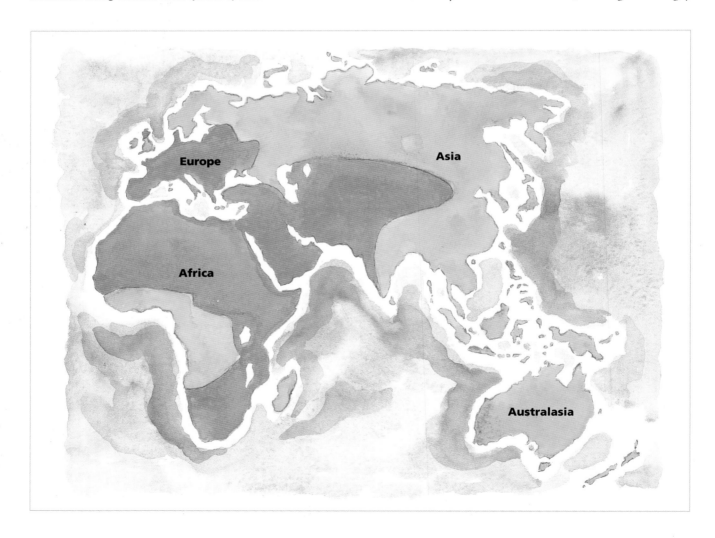

enough it will eat other animals such as insects or even snakes. Its gestation period (about 60 days) is very close to that of the domestic cat, which is another reason it has long been considered the domestic cat's ancestor. Although it is a shy animal, it can easily be domesticated if it is taken when still young, and it will happily live in villages or settlements hunting vermin. The European wildcat, on the other hand, is not easy to domesticate. Even if hand-reared from a kitten, it will remain wild.

The threat of pet cats

Ironically, the greatest threat to the wildcat today, especially across Europe, is its ability to mate with the domestic cat because they are so closely related. In particular, male domestic cats often mate with female wildcats, producing hybridized offspring.

This is obviously most common in areas which are well populated with humans, so that wildcats necessarily live close to humans and their cats; places such as Scotland and large parts of central Europe. This hybridization between wildcats and domestic cats was first noticed at the end of the nineteenth century, when a zoologist examined the pelts of many supposed wildcats and concluded that

many of them must have inherited some genes from the domestic cat population.

Not only can the two species readily mate with one another but, significantly, their offspring will also be fully fertile and able to pass on genes from both parents.

below: **This kitten is half domestic, half wild cat. The domestic cat poses one of the greatest dangers to the survival of the wild cat.**

Domestication

Cats were one of the last animals to be domesticated by man. Hunting and farming communities had long since domesticated animals such as cattle and dogs, but it was not until the population began to move into the towns that the cat became fully domesticated.

It seems that wildcats were originally attracted to towns because as the new settlements started to appear, the cats discovered that there was a good living to be had among the rats, mice, and birds which naturally collect around human settlements. Discarded scraps of food, too, would have tempted the cats, and a town could therefore support a much denser population of cats than the surrounding scrubland or desert.

It wouldn't be long before people came to realize that the cats were their allies. They would hunt the vermin which the people wanted to get rid of, and would also eat the waste food that encouraged the rats and mice.

above: **This wall painting from ancient Egypt shows how cats were used to help with hunting birds.**

above: **The jungle cat's range stretches from Egypt to Vietnam.**

Jungle cats

It seems possible that another wild species of cat entered the equation somewhere around this point. The jungle cat has a range which extends from north Africa, across the Middle East, and into Asia. The Egyptians certainly started to keep jungle cats to hunt wildfowl, but they will also hunt small mammals and other creatures.

Not particularly shy, and easy to domesticate, the jungle cat is not spotted like a wildcat, but has a sandy colored coat similar to that seen in many early Egyptian paintings and in the Abyssinian breed of domestic cat, which many people think is descended directly from the ancient Egyptian cats. It seems possible, therefore, that the domestic cat may have originally been a cross between the African wildcat and the jungle cat. Certainly, whatever their origin, cats were widely domesticated in Egypt by around 2000 BC.

The valuable hunter

The cat owes its domestication to its usefulness as a hunter. It didn't take the ancient Egyptians long to recognize the value of keeping cats near their grain stores to protect their crops from rats after harvesting. And much of the early spread of the domestic cat was owed to its usefulness in controlling vermin on ships, around farms, and in towns and cities.

Cats seem to have become popular as pets quite early on. The ancient Greeks, for example, already used weasels to control vermin but still enjoyed the company of cats. The Romans regarded cats as fireside pets, although they also kept them to keep the rodent population down. The Romans were largely responsible for the spread of domestic cats across Europe.

Sailors and travelers took cats to the Far East, while settlers from Europe brought them to America, Australia, and other parts of the world. Today, most parts of the world have a domestic cat population of some kind, and many have since developed new breeds and exported them back to other places.

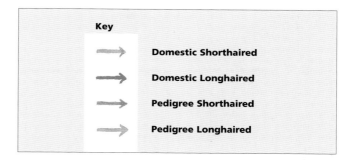

Key

→ Domestic Shorthaired

→ Domestic Longhaired

→ Pedigree Shorthaired

→ Pedigree Longhaired

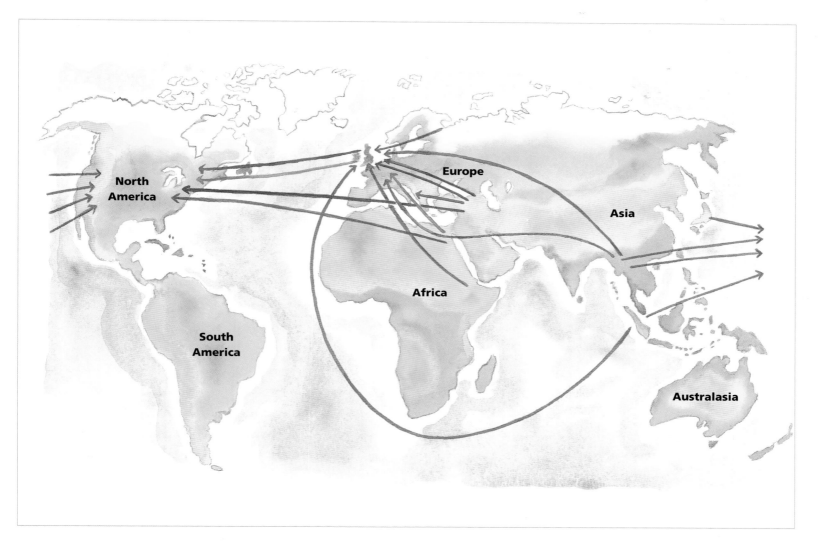

above: **This map illustrates the worldwide spread of domestic cats, and also shows how breeds from both Europe and Asia (originally derived from wildcat lineage) were taken to North America over many centuries.**

C H A P T E R   2

above: **The cat's lack of collarbone increases its stride, helping it sprint faster and allowing it to squeeze into small spaces.**

the biology

of the

cat

The cat's body

The cat has a highly specialized body, evolved to give it the best possible performance as a hunter. It is strong, flexible, and capable of moving very fast. The cat is a mammal and therefore shares many features in common with other mammals. Like all mammals cats have a bony endoskeleton, grow hairs from their skin, produce and suckle live young, and are warm blooded, keeping their bodies at a constant temperature of 101.48° F.

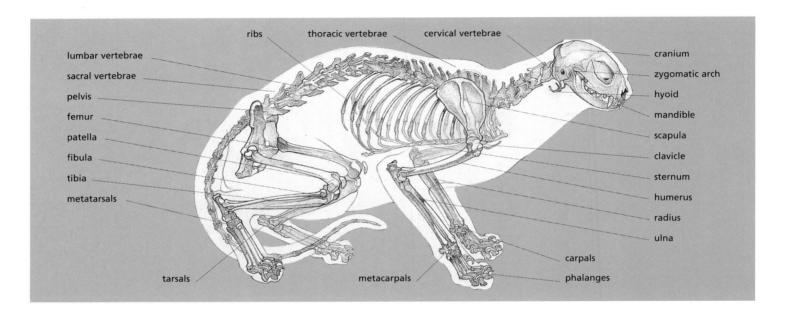

An adult cat weighs between six and 15 pounds. As with all mammals it has a central backbone, which forms the center of its skeleton. This skeleton is made up of over 240 bones—about 40 more than an adult human. Most of the extra bones are contained in the tail and the highly flexible spine. The cat's bones are held together not with ligaments, as in humans, but with muscles—another reason why it is so flexible.

Specialized features

The cat's extra vertebrae help to give it flexibility, but it has other skeletal features which are also highly suited to its life style. It has a shoulder joint which allows the front leg to turn in almost any direction, which means that the cat doesn't need to be able to lift its front leg outward to the side. In turn this means that the cat does not need a collarbone. This is fortunate for the cat because a collarbone has the disadvantage that it makes the chest broader, and the cat needs to keep its body as narrow as possible so that it can squeeze through small spaces. A collarbone would also reduce the length of the cat's stride, which would restrict its ability to sprint fast.

Teeth and claws

The cat's teeth are specialized to enable it to kill and eat meat. It has a group of small incisors at the middle front of the mouth which are used for tearing and scraping. Either side of these are the pairs of large fangs, or canines, which are used to grip the prey as well as to tear. The remaining teeth—premolars and a single pair of molars on each side—are used for cutting the meat into small pieces so it can be digested; unlike humans, cats cannot chew.

Cats' claws are not strictly part of the skeleton, but of the skin. They are made of keratin, which is a protein, and are anchored to the bone in the end of the toe in such a way that they can be easily retracted under a fold of skin.

All four paws have four forward-facing claws, and the two front paws also have a fifth claw which is set further back, and which is used chiefly for climbing and also for holding down prey.

Movement

The fluid movement typical of cats is the result of modified features of the skeleton and muscles. The ends of the bones in the limbs are flatter or rounder than in humans, and covered in cartilage. This allows the bone surfaces, already lubricated with synovial fluid, to glide smoothly over each other. Some joints are adapted so that the socket the end of the bone fits into is very shallow, increasing the cat's freedom of movement.

The two main bones (the femur and tibia) in the cat's hind legs appear to be only loosely connected if you look at the animal's skeleton. In the living cat, however, the joints are connected by specialized cartilage, strong ligaments, and muscles. This means the joint is very stable and able to exert considerable power enabling the cat to jump up to five times its own height. This feature is typical of the cat. Not only are they graceful and swift movers, but they are also exceptionally strong movers because of their extremely powerful muscle system which enables them to sprint, jump, and climb superbly well.

right: **The cat's strong back and hindleg muscles make it an excellent climber. However, it is less well designed for climbing back down.**

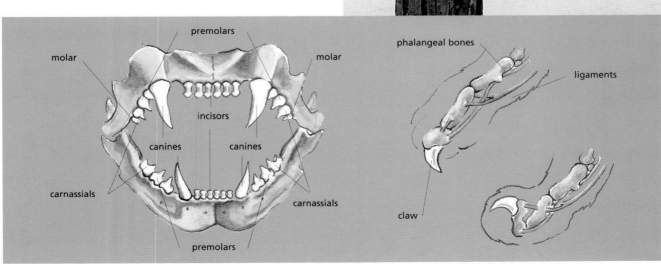

The self-righting reflex

The famous feline attribute of always being able to land on its feet is not wholly accurate, but a falling cat is often able to reposition its body during falling to avoid serious injury on landing. A set of information which reaches the brain from the eyes is combined with impulses from the vestibular apparatus in the ears to transmit an orienting signal to the animal's neck muscles. The head is twisted into an upright and horizontal position and the rest of the body twists and lines itself up accordingly before landing.

above: **Jumping for joy – the cat's skeletal features make it an extremely flexible, powerful animal.**

The secrets of perfect balance

As well as their tremendously flexible backs and their versatility of movement, cats are also first-class balancers. One of the reasons for this is that their muscles are capable of reacting very fast to messages sent via the brain from the eyes and the balancing organs in the inner ear. These muscle reactions are much faster than ours.

The other key reason for the cat's excellent sense of balance is, of course, the tail. This seems to perform the same function as a tightrope-walker's pole—it is a counterbalance. The cat will thrust its tail in the opposite direction to the rest of its body weight to give it stability, which helps it to jump and to corner fast when hunting or being pursued. Cats which have short tails or no tails, such as the Manx, tend to have longer back legs to compensate. But cats which lose their tails in accidents often learn to balance expertly without them, particularly if they are only young when the accident happens.

One of the cat's most famous skills is the ability to fall on its feet. This is a complex skill but, in simplified form, the cat uses its eyes to put its head square with the ground, and the rest of the body then follows. The most frequent injury cats experience when they fall from several stories up is damage to the jaw; their necks are relatively weak and they often cannot prevent their heads from hitting the ground after their feet land.

The cat's coat

A cat's fur helps to protect the skin and it provides a waterproof covering for the cat, as well as keeping it warm. Its fur is not the same all over, but is made up of different types of hair. The longest hairs are known as guard hairs; these are the coarsest, outer hairs and each one grows from a single follicle. Below these hairs is the soft underfur, made up of what are known as secondary hairs.

The color, length, and type of fur varies from breed to breed, with some breeds having no guard hairs at all. The proportion of guard hairs to underfur varies across the body of all cats in any case; there is a much higher proportion of softer underfur on the cat's belly than on its back, for example.

The annual molt

When a cat is cold, tiny muscles near the hair follicles cause the guard hairs to fluff out and make the coat appear thicker. But the cat really does develop a thicker coat in the winter to help keep it warm. Cat's hairs grow at about the same rate as ours, and each follicle grows for a while, then slows, and then stops altogether. After a while the follicle becomes active again—particularly in the spring—and produces a new hair which forces the old hair out, causing molting.

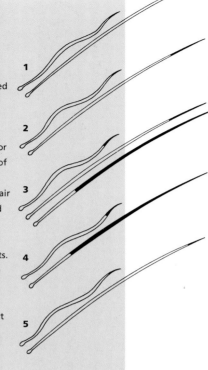

Types of Tipping

In the unusually colored tipped, shaded, and smoke breeds, each effect is produced by a proportion of each hair having a colored tip while the rest of the hair is of a paler color.

1 Tipped cats such as the British Tipped or Chinchilla have tipping at the very ends of the hairs, producing a sparkling effect.

2 Tipping extending further down the hair shaft produces the more strongly colored shaded varieties.

3 Variable bands of color in different areas of the coat give rise to tabby effects.

4 Tipping extending almost to the white hair roots produces the smoke coat in many breeds.

5 In golden varieties, the white base coat of the silver varieties is replaced by a tawny yellow color.

below: **The cat's fur keeps it warm in cold weather and also serves as a waterproof layer.**

Sight

Contrary to popular myth, cats cannot really see in the pitch dark; what they can do is derive the maximum benefit from the smallest amount of light, so their ability to see in very dim light is excellent. Cats have a reflective layer of cells behind the retina so that light bounces to reach the retina a second time. This layer of cells also explains the reflective gleam of a cat's eyes in the dark when the light catches them.

The pupil of a cat's eye, like those of mammals generally, dilates in low light levels and contracts in bright light. Unlike many mammals—and even unlike many other members of the cat family—the domestic cat's pupils contract to a vertical slit rather than a round pinprick. This is even more efficient for closing down the pupil than a round shape; the cat needs this efficiency in order to protect its highly sensitive reflective retina.

above: **In bright light, the cat's pupil narrows right down to protect the retina.**

far right: **A layer of reflective cells at the back of the eye makes the cat's eyes gleam distinctively in the dark.**

Inside the eye

The slightly egg-shaped eye is surrounded by the tough sclera, replaced at the front by the transparent cornea, behind which the aqueous humor protects the iris and pupil. Jellylike vitreous humor fills the cavity behind the lens, and at the back of the eye is the light-sensitive retina, and the reflective *tapetum lucidum*. The optic nerve transmits signals from the eye to the brain.

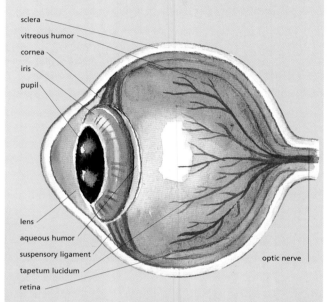

sclera
vitreous humor
cornea
iris
pupil
lens
aqueous humor
suspensory ligament
tapetum lucidum
retina
optic nerve

Vision

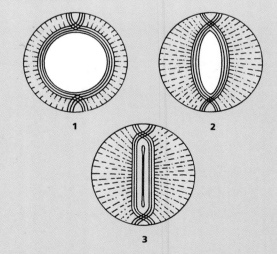

1

2

3

1 Changes in the size and shape of the pupil generally relate to the amount of light entering the eye. In darkness the pupil dilates.
2 In natural diffused daylight the pupil is seen as a normal vertical oval shape.
3 In very low light, the pupil closes down to a narrow slit with an enlarged orifice at each end.

Getting the full picture

Cats have a much wider field of vision than we do. They can see a total field of about 285 degrees, of which 130 degrees are binocular (seen with both eyes). This binocular vision enables them to assess distance and length clearly, which gives them great accuracy when hunting.

When it comes to color vision, it is thought that a cat's eyes are capable of seeing colors but, interestingly, the cat's brain does not recognize them. Cats can occasionally be trained to identify colors, but without training they simply don't perceive them. In order to be a cat, it just isn't necessary to distinguish colors.

Hearing

Cats can distinguish the location of two sounds which are very close together in direction because of their highly adapted ears. The external ear does not simply act as a funnel; its surface is irregular, which allows it to identify the source of a sound very precisely. This ability is enhanced even more by the fact that the cat has a wide range of ear movements; it can turn its ears through 180 degrees and point them toward the sound that it hears.

A cat's outer ear contains 30 muscles, compared to only six in the human external ear.

Cats need to be able to hear the sounds emitted by their prey, especially small rodents and birds. Consequently, cats are particularly well adapted to be able to hear high-pitched noises. They can hear sounds as much as two octaves above the human range—and higher than a dog's range. However, the lowest frequency they can hear is not as low as humans' or dogs' frequency range.

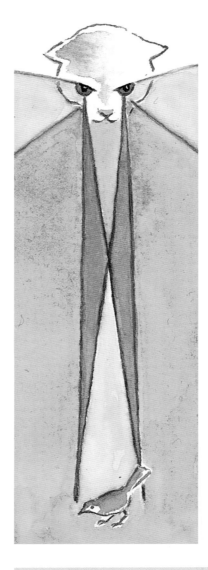

left: **Both eyes face forward allowing the fields of vision to overlap. This produces stereoscopic sight and enables the hunting cat's accurate assessment of distance and prey location.**

below left: **Sensitive hearing is a vital attribute for a creature that survives by hunting.**

Anatomy of an ear

Sound waves are funneled down the external auditory canal to the ear drum. In the middle ear, weak vibrations are turned into stronger vibrations. Nerve signals are then sent along the auditory nerve to the brain.

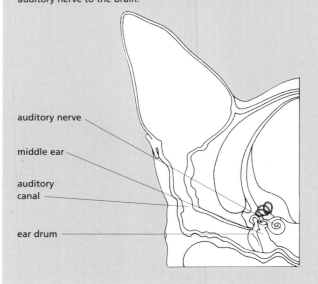

auditory nerve

middle ear

auditory canal

ear drum

Touch

A cat's sense of touch is not as highly developed as some of its other senses, except in certain sensitive areas. The most touch-sensitive parts of a cat's body are the parts which are not covered in fur but are bare skin, especially the nose and the pads of the paws.

A cat will use its nose to assess the temperature of food as well as smelling it before it eats, and its nose is very sensitive to touch as well as temperature. It will also investigate a new object using the paw pads. Often it will reach out one paw to touch an object gingerly, and then more firmly, before investigating it with its nose. Cats do not generally like to have their pads stroked or touched, and this may well be because they are so sensitive.

The cat's whiskers

No one is certain exactly what the function of whiskers is, although they are clearly important. If you remove a cat's whiskers you will disorient it for quite some time. It used to be thought that the longest whiskers were the same width as the cat's body, so that the cat could use them to judge whether it could fit through a space. However, this simply isn't true, and the length of a cat's whiskers does not correlate to the size of its body.

The cat seems to use its whiskers as antennae: if it moves with its head low to the ground in the dark, its whiskers will warn it if there are stones or holes in its path. It is also thought that if the whiskers make contact with the cat's prey in the dark, it can react so fast that it will catch the prey before it has a chance to escape.

above: **Cats often use their paw pads to pick up clues as to the identity of a new object.**

above: **Cats can bend their whiskers downwards, which may help to guide them over uneven ground in the dark.**

below: **Cats use their noses to assess the temperature of food and to smell it before eating.**

above: **Cats rub their heads against objects and people to mark them with scent from their scent glands.**

Smell

The cat's well-developed sense of smell helps it to hunt, and to recognize scents such as those of its own kittens or of its owner. It can identify different scents within its regular territory. Cats will also use their sense of smell to pick out their own scent-marks and those of other cats. Every time your cat rubs itself against your legs or head-butts you in greeting, it is leaving its scent mark on you. Spraying—which is more common and more pungent in unneutered toms—is a much stronger form of scent-marking.

If a cat needs to detect faint or important scents, it will often curl back its lips and open its mouth in a grimace known as the flehmen reaction. This facial expression allows the cat to catch scents on the tongue and then transfer them to the Jacobson's organ on the roof of the mouth, which relays information about the scent to the brain. "Flehming" is often used by tom cats on the scent of a female on heat. You might also observe it in a cat which has been moved to a new territory, such as when you move house.

Flehmen Reaction

This is exhibited when the cat is confronted by chemicals in smells, either of sexual origin or from musky odors. Airborne molecules are trapped on the tongue which is flicked back to press on the opening of the Jacobson's organ. Information is relayed to the brain's hypothalamus, which dictates the cat's response.

The cat exhibiting the flehmen reaction stretches its neck, opens its mouth, and curls back its upper lips in a snarl. It may be so affected by a smell that it also starts salivating.

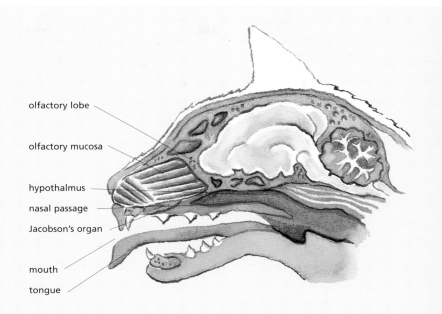

olfactory lobe

olfactory mucosa

hypothalmus

nasal passage

Jacobson's organ

mouth

tongue

Good and bad smells

Cats are very sensitive to smells which contain nitrogen compounds. This sensitivity is important because food which is starting to go off generally emits nitrogen-rich chemicals. Other smells, however, attract as strongly as this deters. One of the cat's most famous favorite smells is the herb catnip (*Nepeta cataria*). This happens to give off a scent which is very similar to that excreted in the urine of female cats, which is why tom cats, especially, are attracted to catnip.

below: **Catnip (*Nepeta cataria*) has an extraordinary effect on cats of both sexes. Toms can be particularly affected, however, because the herb gives off a scent similar to that excreted by sexually active females.**

Taste

Cats in the wild are pure carnivores, and their sense of taste has evolved to suit this diet. They are exceptionally rare among animals in that they have little or no response to sweet things. As meat eaters, of course, they would not need to develop a taste for sweet foods. Curiously, domestic cats do have a few taste receptors on the tongue which respond to sweet foods, and the number is on the increase—perhaps an adaptation to domestic life.

However, cats have a very strong response to the taste of water, and this taste seems to mask any sweet taste

which they detect. Some limited ability to detect sweetness ought to be useful to cats, since they have a very low tolerance to sugar, and presumably it would therefore be useful to recognize it in order to avoid it.

Coping without taste

Cats can lose their sense of taste either temporarily or permanently if they contract a respiratory illness. In any case, it tends to deteriorate with age. But taste and smell are very closely linked, and cats seem to identify different kinds of meat by smell rather than by taste. They can certainly tell different meats apart, which may explain why they can have such strong opinions about which foods they will and won't eat.

left: **Cats are pure carnivores, responsible for killing millions of birds per year.**

below: **Cats have a very strong response to the taste of water.**

CHAPTER 3

above: **Cats were first domesticated, and allowed to live in houses, in Egyptian times.**

the cat and man

Cats in Ancient Egypt

The Egyptians and the local wildcats had a mutually beneficial arrangement. The Egyptian towns which were springing up provided excellent hunting and scavenging opportunities for the African wildcats and jungle cats; meanwhile the Egyptians were delighted to find that the cats were keeping down the local rodent population for them. They encouraged the cats, who responded enthusiastically, and in time the cats became domesticated.

above: **Egyptian tomb painting from the 1st Dynasty, depicting cats herding geese.**

The cats were encouraged to protect the grain stores from rats and mice, and the jungle cats were also trained to hunt wildfowl for the Egyptians. But how exactly did the cat go from being a domestic animal to being a god? Its divine status in Egypt has led to four thousand years of being alternately deified and vilified in cultures around the globe. But how did it all start?

The Egyptians, like many other cultures, worshipped lions. It doesn't take much to see that if you share your habitat with lions you have to treat them with great respect, and this is a very typical way for cultures to create animal deities. Nearby Babylonia, for example, worshipped the lion as a symbol of power, and associated it with their goddess Ishtar. Imagine the Egyptians' amazement, then, to find that they could domesticate the miniature version of one of their great gods. The cat, through its relationship with the lion, became associated with all of the lion's divine attributes.

left: **Egyptian lion goddess. The worship of the cat was a direct result of the worship of lions.**

Divine status

The cat quickly became a sacred animal and was treated with enormous respect. Killing a cat, even by accident, was often punishable by death. In fact, it was so unthinkable to harm a cat that it gave King Cambyses of Persia, in the fifth century BC, his chance to conquer Egypt. He devised the ingenious ruse of having his army attach live cats to the front of their shields when they attacked. The unfortunate Egyptians were unable to retaliate for fear of harming the sacred animals and were left with no option but surrender.

Most Egyptian families kept their own cat. When the cat died, the family would go into mourning and would ritually shave off their eyebrows. The eyebrows may well have symbolized the cat's fur. In any case the gesture served as a sign that the family cat had died.

Egypt was conquered by the Romans in 30 BC, but the new rulers allowed the Egyptians to continue to worship their own gods including Bastet, the cat goddess, whose cult had become huge. It wasn't until AD 392 that the Christian emperor, Theodosius, outlawed the Egyptians' indigenous cults and religious practices, and declared Christianity the state religion. The cat's reign was over, and for the next two thousand years it would find its relationship with man far more precarious.

below: **A battle scene depicting the King of Persia, Cambyses II (522 BC) defeating the Egyptians at Pelusium. Realizing the extent of the Egyptians' reverence for cats, Cambyses captured several of the animals and used them as shields. The Egyptians, reluctant to wound the cats, surrendered the city to him.**

The cult of Bastet

Bastet was the great Egyptian cat goddess, around whom one of the greatest Egyptian cults grew up. Originally she was simply one aspect of the moon goddess Isis, but her following increased to such an extent that at the height of her popularity she was even more important than Isis herself.

Cats were associated with the moon in ancient Egypt —and have been ever since. Part of the reason for this is that they often hunt at night, and their reflective eyes seem to resemble the moon. Also the great sun god Ra was associated with the lion—that strong, golden-colored creature whose power symbolized the sun. It stood to reason then that the cat—a lesser version of the lion— should symbolize the moon, a lesser version of the sun.

Bastet was also known as Bast or Pasht (which is thought to be the origin of the word "puss"). She was generally represented as either a giant cat or as a woman with the head of a cat. She was often surrounded by kittens, or carried a basket full of them. She was also a fertility goddess, as moon goddesses tend to be because of the link between the moon's monthly cycle and women's similar cycle. She also carried a shield (or *egis*), which symbolized her protective powers.

Bastet was usually depicted carrying a sistrum, which was a kind of rattle used by women to scare off evil spirits. The sistrum has four strings and this is probably the source of the traditional rhyme, "Hey diddle diddle, the cat and the fiddle." (The cow jumping over the moon is Hathor, the cow-headed moon goddess.)

Worshipping the cat

The center of the cult of Bastet was a city in the Nile delta called Bubastis. The temple at Bubastis dates from about 2500 BC and was an impressive site, set on an island with no access except for a single entrance passage. Bastet's cult grew until, in 945 BC, Bubastis was made the capital city of Egypt, and Bastet was given precedence over all other goddesses in the Egyptian pantheon. Every year, a great festival would be held and people would make the pilgrimage along the Nile to attend. Among other rituals, sacrifices of young cats would be made.

Bubastis is the site of Egypt's most famous cat cemetery. Cat cemeteries have also been found elsewhere in Egypt, including at Giza, where Cheops built the largest pyramid. It seems that many of the mummified cats which have been unearthed were the victims of sacrifice, since they had had their necks broken. Most were young—not yet fully grown—and may well have been bred especially for the purpose.

left: **Bronze statue of the goddess Bastet, on a rectangular base, dating from the Ptolemaic age. She has a basket on the crook of her left arm, containing kittens, and an egis or shield in her left hand. In her right hand she holds a heavy Hathor-handled sistrum. She wears a striped dress with a fringed and pleated edge to the skirt.**

far left: **Egyptian bronze cat from Dynasty XXVI. Around its neck there is a bead necklace from which is suspended an egis of Bastet. The ears are pierced where earrings would once have been.**

right: **The cat was very important to the Egyptians, and many statues and paintings of cats still survive.**

below: **Egyptian cat coffins seen in two halves and as a whole. The mummified cats that were placed in these were sacrificial cats, usually young and possibly bred specifically for that purpose.**

Although Bastet was the cause of the cat's greatest period of worship, she was probably also the cause of the animal's decline to persecution and cruelty in later centuries. Her associations with women, and especially with the moon, led to the cat's subsequent association with the black arts and its demonization by Christians.

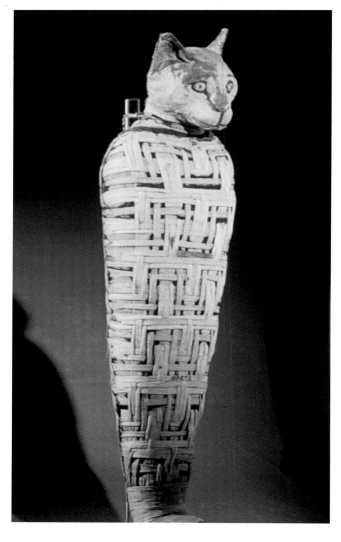

above right: **Remains at the site of the temple at Bubastis, center of the cat cult of Bastet. The temple dates from about 2500 BC.**

right: **Egyptian cat mummy. Mummified cats appear to have been the victims of sacrifice.**

The spread of the cat

Up until about 500 or 600 BC, the domestic cat was restricted to Egypt. Then it started to reach the classical world. It seems that a few cats were traded with the Greeks, although trade did not become widespread until Christianity reached Egypt.

Once the Romans arrived in Egypt, the movement of cats to other parts of the Roman Empire increased. The Romans seem to have adopted some of the Egyptians' attitude to cats, and treated them reverently. As well as using them to control rats and mice, they also kept them as house pets.

The spread of cats through the rest of western and northern Europe seems to have followed the advances of the Roman Empire. There are two possible ways in which this could have happened—or both may have occurred simultaneously. One explanation is that the Romans took cats with them on their travels, presumably to control vermin; the other is that the cats followed the Romans of their own accord, since the brown rat and the house mouse were both expanding their territories across the Roman Empire.

Certainly we know that the domestic cat made it as far as Britain along with the Romans in the first century BC, because there are several instances of evidence for their presence there. Domestic cats spread beyond the borders of the Roman Empire to the rest of Europe, all the way into Scandinavia.

above: **This glazed earthenware cat was probably a good luck charm. It is Egyptian, from the Roman period (1st century AD).**

top: **A Roman gravestone from the 1st or 2nd century AD, found in Britain, shows a child with a pet cat.**
above: **Clay tiles, from a Roman tile factory in Britain, show that a cat was walking through the yard while the tiles were still drying.**

Cats in the East

The domestic cat had certainly reached India and China by around AD 400; it seems that cats were traded along the Silk Route which ran from the Mediterranean through Persia, north of the Himalayas, and into northern China. This was the key trading route to the East for centuries, and cats would have been of value to the Chinese and Indians for vermin control, just as they were elsewhere.

It appears that Buddhist monks adopted cats to guard their temples very soon after the cat's introduction to the East, and it was the Buddhists who took cats to Japan with them in the sixth century AD.

Around the world, cats took many of the myths and folk tales they had acquired in Egypt with them, and therefore continued to hold many of the same associations. For example, the cat was a symbol of fertility in the East just as it had been in Egypt. Cats were luckier in the East, however, than in the West. They were never demonized as they were by Christians and were revered in many places, not only in Buddhist temples.

above: **Cats are found in Buddhist temples where they are used as guards.**

below: **A mid-19th century print of cat merchants and tea dealers on the quayside at Tong-Chon in China.**

left: **Settlers leaving Europe for North America. Cats often accompanied their owners on their new life.**
below: **A Calusa cat figure; the Calusa were one of the native peoples of Florida.**

American cats

Cats didn't reach the United States, of course, until it was settled. Christopher Columbus may have taken cats with him on his first voyage to America in 1492. It is recorded that he certainly took them on his second visit in 1493–95. Interestingly, the Spanish settlers in the south of North America, and the British and French settlers in the north, brought their own cats with them. This led to two independent populations of domestic cat. Even today, genetic profiling shows predominantly English-type cats in the northeast of the USA, and predominantly Spanish genes in the cats of the southern states.

The cat as god and demon

It all goes back to the Egyptians, as is so often the case with cats. The cat acquired many religious and spiritual associations through the part it played in the Egyptian pantheon. It became associated with the moon, with women, and with fertility. Through its connection with the moon and darkness, it was thought to be concerned with the unconscious and therefore the hidden.

It's not hard to see how this could be interpreted in significantly varying lights. In a society which regards women with great respect—and treats fertility as important and praiseworthy—the cat is revered as a noble and even divine animal. Many cultures, too, expect their gods to behave in mysterious and inexplicable ways and a connection with the moon, with its sense of the dark and the hidden, simply makes the cat more godlike.

On the other hand, in a male-dominated society such as those of the Western Dark Ages and Middle Ages, fertility can be dangerously associated with sex and is therefore to be covered up and not discussed. Add to this attitude a view of god as monotheistic and the belief that the hidden side of things is dark and evil, and you have set the stage for the persecution of cats in the name of religion.

above: *The cat gets its paws under the table.* Courting couple with pet cat at their feet, c.1887. It was only after the first cat show in Britain, held in 1871, that cats became once again accepted as pets.

The cat as a pet

It took a long time for cats in the West to recover from their association with witches and regain the position of affectionate companion which they had held in Egypt and ancient Rome. In America the recovery took longer since the Pilgrim Fathers had brought a strong anti-witchcraft attitude with them when they settled. Apart from the few cats which had arrived in America with the early settlers of the fifteenth century, cats had a minimal presence for a very long time.

It wasn't until the middle of the eighteenth century that cats began to rise in people's estimations once again. Those of a more enlightened mind dismissed the notion that cats were agents of the devil and began to recognize their charms at last. The English literary figure Dr. Samuel Johnson was one of the best known cat owners of the time, possessing several cats, the best-known being a cat by the name of Hodge.

Things began to change slowly but the cat was still regarded by many with suspicion. In Victorian times, the

number of feral cats in towns and cities outweighed the number of house cats by a long way. It wasn't until the first cat show, held in Britain in 1871, that the cat really began to be accepted once again as a pet.

above: **The memorial to Dr. Samuel Johnson's cat, Hodge, in London, England.**

left: **Street-trader selling pet food in Victorian England, c.1895.**

The twentieth-century cat

Things have changed over the last hundred years and we now go to almost the opposite extreme in our attitude to cats. It is only about two hundred years since they were persecuted in the West; now organizations exist to protect them and to rescue injured or feral cats.

Far from banishing them from the house, we now cosset and pamper our cats—who are more than happy to go along with this approach! We buy them special food, and some of us even try to discourage them from following their natural hunting instincts. One study in the USA found that one third of all domestic cats were overweight, suggesting that we are now killing them with kindness where once we killed them with cruelty.

Far from being embarrassed or even afraid to own a cat, as might have been the case a few centuries ago, we now go out of our way to groom and show our cats. We even breed kittens which, in the case of pedigrees, can fetch high prices and earn us kudos.

When our cats finally die, many of them are buried in cemeteries, especially in America—an echo perhaps of the cat cemeteries of ancient Egypt.

Even modern science supports our new-found enthusiasm for the cat. Many studies have shown that living with a cat can improve our health. Pet owners live longer than non-pet owners, and it has now been shown that stroking a cat or other pet reduces stress levels and even lowers blood pressure.

below: **Cats are now known to be ideal companions for the elderly.**

below right: **We now go out of our way to groom and show cats, such as this Turkish Van cat shown here with her three six week-old kittens.**

below left: **Pet cemetery, California. Cats are now so well regarded that cemeteries have been created for us in which to bury our beloved pets.**

far right: **In the lap of luxury—Western Society now fully welcomes cats into the home.**

The image of the cat

But the cat's true nature still shows through and is perhaps the reason many of us choose to live with cats. Even a pedigree cat living in an apartment is obviously related to the wild creatures that cats once were. Of all domestic animals, the cat is by far the most successful at surviving in the wild. A house cat can turn feral very easily and get by extremely well compared with other animals. Cat owners know that their cats are still very close to their wilder side. They are independent and opportunistic—as a successful hunter needs to be—and it may be this that partly explains their attraction. We feel deeply flattered when a cat agrees to live with us, because we know it has a choice. It could walk out of the door at any time and look after itself if it wished.

The cat has never lost its ancient image. You only have to look at the way cats are used in advertising to see this. They are almost always associated with women rather than men, and often with sexuality and therefore sensual luxury. Cats are also linked with the night, witchcraft, and superstition even today, and are used in commercials to convey a sense of mystery. Even in the twentieth century the cat still carries with it many of the associations it collected 4,000 years ago in ancient Egypt.

above: **Here a kitten adds charm to a 1960s fashion advertisement, and** right: **It's love of comfort leads it to be used as a symbol of warmth and luxury.**

below: **The cat's association with witchcraft have never been forgotten.**

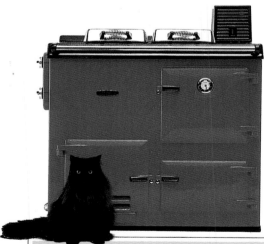

THE WORLD'S BEST-LOOKING COOKER.

above: **The cat's darker side is used in this 1970's advertisment for a popular tobacco brand.**

CHAPTER 4

above: **Cats have a natural mystical quality which has given them a firm place in the myths and legends of many cultures.**

the cat in myth and legend

The symbolism of cats

Four thousand years ago, the cat began to find its way into myth and legend from its base in ancient Egypt. It came to represent specific things to the Egyptians: it was associated with certain concepts and behaviors. By the time the domestic cat began to enlarge its range beyond Egypt, it had acquired broad symbolism which began to spread out across the world.

above: **The moon-like eyes of the cat have inevitably caused much of its traditional symbolism.**

Some of the cat's associations derived from its basic nature and others from the particular myths which had grown up around it and its place in Egyptian mythology. Either way, it is possible to see particular themes surfacing again and again in worldwide myths originating in Scandinavia or China, Ireland or India, and it is obvious that cats will always be connected with these themes.

The moon

Cats are deeply associated with the moon because their eyes resemble it when they are caught in the light at night and appear to wax and wane like the moon as the pupils dilate and constrict. Also, because lions represent the sun, so the cat—a little lion—represents the moon—a little sun. The moon is the cat's central symbolic association.

The unconscious

The sun symbolizes the open, light consciousness. So the moon, its night-time counterpart, symbolizes the opposite: the hidden, dark unconscious. In Eastern terms, the sun is Yang and the moon is Yin. The cat, through its connection with the moon, takes on these connotations.

The cat goddess Bastet was the moon goddess, and was often depicted as the left eye of Horus, the solar god (his right eye was her sister Sekhmet, the lion-headed goddess). The left eye—and the left side of the body—is governed by the intuitive right hemisphere of the brain.

below: **The yin-yang symbol, central to Eastern philosophy. Cats are associated with yin: the dark, night-time, unconscious world.**

The feminine connection

Once again the cat is linked, through its association with the moon, to other lunar symbols. The moon, and therefore the cat, is strongly associated with women because women's menstrual cycle is seen to mirror the moon's monthly cycle through the heavens. Again, this symbolism dates back to ancient Egypt.

above and below: **It is four thousand years since cats became part of Egyptian culture, yet they are still associated primarily with women (Carole Lombard above, and Eartha Kitt below). They are thought to lend the women an air of mystery.**

above: **Female cats make excellent mothers, and produce about 4–6 kittens in a litter, so their reputation for fertility is well-deserved.**

Fertility

It's not hard to see that, once you've identified a link between the moon and the menstrual cycle, the moon (and its symbol the cat) should also be linked with fertility. Added to this, cats are prolific breeders, which helps to support this connection. The Egyptians linked the cat strongly with birth. Their hieroglyph for birth (*ru*) was a simple depiction of the shape of a cat's eye, representing a doorway or opening. This symbolizes both the birth canal and the gateway from the spiritual plane (governed by the moon) into the physical plane.

The Egyptians had another hieroglyph, the *tau* cross, meaning time in the physical plane. The two hieroglyphs were combined, the *ru* set on top of the *tau* cross, to create the *ankh* symbol, which signifies life and immortality. This symbol was adapted to represent Venus, the Roman goddess of beauty who symbolized the archetypal woman—and whose *ankh* symbol therefore incorporates the cat's eye.

Eternity

Eternity is traditionally represented by an unbroken circle with no beginning and no end. The circle means enlightenment to Zen Buddhists; for the Chinese, their Yin-Yang symbol forms a circle representing eternity. When a cat sleeps, its nose and tail often touch, creating an unbroken circle. It is this habit that has led to their association with eternity.

left: **Sekhmet, the lion-headed goddess, holding the ankh symbol.**

below: **The cat creates an unbroken circle, traditionally associated with eternity, when it sleeps nose to tail.**

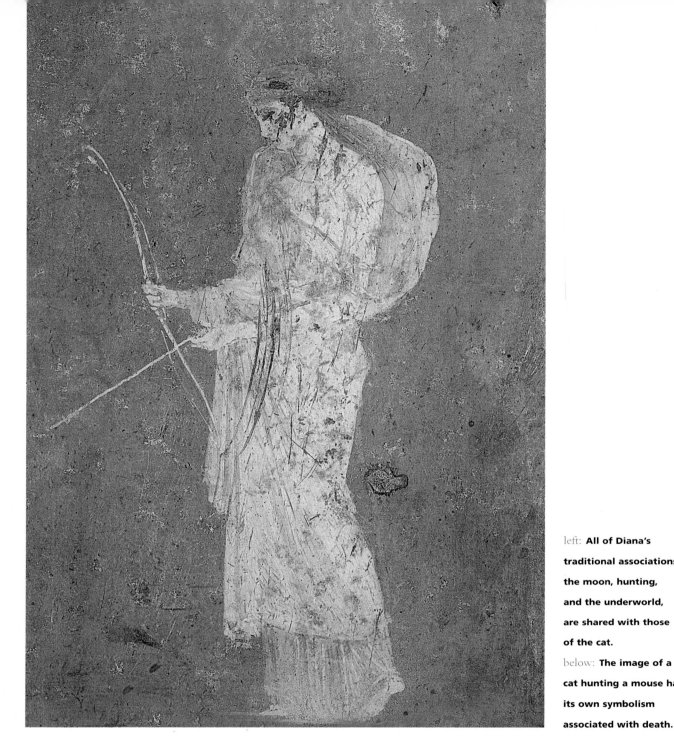

Death

The Romans' moon goddess was Diana, but as their mythology developed she became a triple goddess, acquiring three aspects. She was known as Luna in the heavens, Diana in her earthly form, and Hecate in the underworld (when the moon disappeared from view). All three of these aspects were associated with cats, but the one which lent the cat its association with death was Hecate. Hecate—originally a Greek goddess who was incorporated into Roman myth—ruled over the dead in the underworld. Interestingly, this link also explains why many moon goddesses, such as the Norse Freya, were also goddesses of the dead or at least of men slain in battle.

The image of a cat hunting a mouse is often symbolic. The mouse represents the human soul and the cat symbolizes death, playing with the mouse before finally killing it. In parts of Europe, mice were considered to be the souls of the dead and people would even put out food for them.

Freedom

This is one cat association which has not been traced back as far as ancient Egypt but seems to date from classical times. The Greek goddess Artemis and the Roman Diana were the later counterparts of Bastet and therefore took on her symbols including the cat. They were both moon goddesses, and also goddesses of the hunt and of freedom, wildness, and nature. The Romans therefore used the cat as a symbol of liberty, not least because its independent nature made it so appropriate for the role. It was subsequently used in heraldry to represent the same thing. The Vandals and the Dutch, among others, both used the cat in their emblems. The Dutch fought so hard for their liberty that once they achieved it they adopted the cat as their symbol in recognition.

Watchfulness

The Egyptian moon goddess Bastet spent each night gazing down from the heavens, just as a cat can sit for hours watching through a window, or tracking a bird. So the cat came to symbolize detached watchfulness.

below: **Reluctant Playmate** by Horatio Henry Cowdery shows two playful kittens learning to hunt.

Stealth

Cats are stealthy hunters, as well as being wily, resourceful, and inquisitive. These qualities are so strong that the cat has become one of the chief symbols of this kind of behavior. Back in the sixth century BC Aesop cast the cat as a trickster. Puss-in-Boots is another traditional example of a cat who is resourceful and wily.

below: **The cat's intrinsic nature hasn't changed over the centuries, and nor has its symbolism and associations. Here, in a page from Caxton's _Æsop_ printed in 1474, it is the hunter meting out death.**

below left: **The story of Puss-in-Boots is a classic example of the cat being portrayed as clever and resourceful. Here, Puss asks his master for a pair of boots and a game bag.**

The Egyptians

Since cat mythology started in Egypt, this is the place to begin a tour of cats in myth and legend. As well as Bastet there was another Egyptian deity who was also represented as a cat: the god Ra.

Ra was originally symbolized by the lion, but came to be represented in other forms such as with the head of a hawk, a solar disc, and a serpent, or with the head of a ram. But at night, he often took the form of the Great Cat.

A typical example of this is in the myth of Ra and Apep, the Great Serpent.

This is a myth to explain the eternal cycle of night and day. Both the creatures involved, the cat and the serpent, represent eternity because both can form a complete unbroken circle, nose to tail. Ra takes the form of a cat because the cat is associated with the night, the time of the moon. During the day he often takes the form of a lion, but never the form of the Great Cat. Occasionally Apep would manage to swallow Ra's solar barge (this would explain eclipses) but the Great Cat would always win in the end.

left: **Cats are still as common a sight in modern Egypt as they were in ancient times.**
below: **Egyptian bronze from c.600BC of a lactating cat and her tiny kittens.**

The Cat and the Serpent

Each morning Ra, the sun god, begins his journey across the sky, above the twelve regions of Egypt, in his great solar barge. He looks down in judgment on the people of Egypt until, as night falls, he reaches the entrance to the underworld.

The underworld has twelve caverns, each populated by the dead, who see daylight only during the single hour that Ra passes through their cavern.

Ra's ancient enemy, the serpent Apep, lives in the underworld and waits for Ra every night. He spends the twelve hours of darkness wrestling with Ra to bring him down, or even halting the barge by drinking all the water beneath it. But Ra assumes the form of the Great Cat and cuts off Apep's head.

So each morning, Ra once again appears safely ready to journey across the sky.

Nine lives

The Egyptians are also responsible for the association between cats and the number nine. Nine is a sacred number in many religions; it is three times three, and many cultures worshipped trinities. The Egyptian cultural center of Heliopolis had nine gods associated with it, each of whom was associated in some way with cats.

This is almost certainly the link between cats and the number nine, which has since given rise to many practices and beliefs, most notably the belief that cats have nine lives. It was also a common belief at one time that witches could transform themselves into cats nine times in their lives.

left: **The cat has long been associated with the sacred number nine.**

below: **It was once believed that witches could transform themselves into cats, as depicted in this woodcut, c.1650.**

Classical cats

When the Greeks built up their own mythology, they borrowed many aspects of it from neighboring cultures. One of the most important of these was the culture of Egypt. Consequently, many Greek gods are almost direct developments of Egyptian gods. Since one of the most important Egyptian gods was Bastet, it's no surprise that she was transferred to Greek myth and legend. She became Artemis.

Artemis was the Greek goddess of the moon, who also became associated with the hunt, nature, and freedom. Her borrowed link with the cat may well have contributed to her association with hunting, since cats are such accomplished hunters. Artemis was the twin sister of Apollo, the sun god, perpetuating the role of the moon as a lesser—and feminine—aspect of the sun. There is an echo of the link with Egypt in the Greek myth of Typhon.

She wasn't the only one. The darker side of Artemis was represented by a different goddess: Hecate, a wild moon goddess who dated back to pre-Hellenic Greece. Hecate had been absorbed into Greek mythology as an aspect of Artemis and she, too, transformed herself into a cat.

The ancient Greeks had long associated lions with fertility and with the underworld.

When they discovered cats they gave them many of the same associations. One of these was a connection with water—statues of lions often guarded their springs and fountains. Although cats dislike water, this connection with it lingered and in many cultures cats were associated with the ability to bring, or prevent, rain. This was probably strengthened by their link with fertility, since rain is essential for the fertility of crops.

The Greek gods lived on Mount Olympus. But they were threatened by the monster Typhon and in fear they all fled to Egypt. However, they were still afraid that Typhon would find them, so they decided to assume disguises in order to hide from him. Each god took the form of an animal; Artemis transformed herself into a cat.

above: **When the ancient Greeks discovered cats, they accorded them many of the attributes they had long associated with lions.**
left: **Graeco-Roman bronze figure of a seated cat.**

above: **The goddess Diana and Endymion, by Luca Giordano (1632–1705).**

The Roman cat goddesses

Artemis was adopted by the Romans and transformed into their triple moon goddess, Diana (whose other aspects were Luna and Hecate). Diana, who also acquired the associations with hunting and with wildness and freedom, was often depicted with a cat at her feet to symbolize liberty. The story of the gods' flight to Egypt persisted into Roman legend and, in the updated version, Diana still transformed herself into a cat.

Diana took the form of a cat in order to mate with her brother, Lucifer, god of light. They produced a daughter, Aradia, who was a teacher of witchcraft. It's fairly clear that when Christians began to demonize the pagan religions, the Greek and Roman moon goddesses were seen as the leaders of the witches ... along with their cat familiars.

Cats in China

The cat's association with human fertility often led to it being associated with the fertility of the land and its crops. The Chinese god of agriculture, Li-Shou, took the form of a cat and was worshipped by peasant farmers who made sacrifices to him at the end of the harvest. Clearly the cat's ability to protect the harvested grain from rats and mice was another reason for invoking a cat god. The third connection between cats and the harvest is that crops were traditionally planted according to the phases of the moon.

The Chinese also believed that cats were able to bring people back from the dead—as zombies. There are probably two reasons for this, which are connected. One is that cats are, of course, associated with death and the underworld. They would have brought this association all the way from Egypt with them, via the Mediterranean. And the other reason is that the crops themselves die down and go below ground for the winter, only to be reborn in the spring. In many mythologies the gods or goddesses of the underworld are also responsible for the harvest, including the Egyptian god Osiris, who was ruler of the underworld and judge of the dead.

Certainly, the Chinese associated cats with death and (partial) rebirth. They were wary of them even though they worshipped Li-Shou. They were careful to keep their cats well away from the dead before they were buried.

below: **The cat was introduced to China along the famous Silk Route. It brought with it much of its mythical tradition from ancient Egypt. This facsimile of the *Papyrus of Ani* depicts the adoration of Osiris from the *Book of the Dead*.**

Cats in Southeast Asia

In both Siam (now Thailand) and Burma (Myanmar), sacred cats were kept in the Buddhist temples as guardians. Each of these countries had its own breed of cat; the Siamese and the Birman (not to be confused with the Burmese).

The Buddhist people believed that when people died, their souls transmigrated into the bodies of cats. This obviously made cats sacred, because they weren't necessarily cats at all but human souls occupying a cat's body. Members of the royal family of Siam used to be interred in a burial chamber whose roof contained small holes. A live cat would be buried with them.

If the cat managed to escape, this was seen as a sign that the spirit of the buried member of the royal family had passed into the cat.

The cat in Eastern astrology

There are two different legends in the East about the reason that the cat is not included in the twelve signs of the Eastern zodiac (see panel below).

below left: **The cat's liking for taking a nap excluded it from the Chinese zodiac.**

below: **Female blue-point Birman–a sacred breed in Burma.**

1) When the Buddha died, every creature arrived to witness his entry to Nirvana except for the cat which, unfortunately, failed to turn up because it had stopped on the way to take a nap. As a punishment for this appalling behaviour, the cat was excluded from the zodiac.

2) The animals of the world all gathered at the Buddha's death to see him admitted to Nirvana. The cat was present along with the rest of the animals. However, the cat and the serpent were the only two creatures who didn't weep at the Buddha's passing (perhaps, both representing eternity, they alone recognized that death was simply a stage in an eternal cycle). Then a tiny mouse scuttled over to the oil lamp beside the Buddha's body and began to lick up the oil.

The cat responded instantly and the mouse was killed. But the Buddha had forbidden that any animal should be killed and the cat, by disregarding this instruction at the worst possible time, was punished with exclusion from the zodiac.

Japanese cat myth

Cats arrived in Japan in the sixth century AD. Because they were introduced as sacred animals by the Buddhist monks they were generally held in high esteem by the Japanese, and have always had protected status.

When the tenth-century Emperor Ichijo forbade using cats as working animals, there were terrible repercussions. The problem was the silk industry. Mice were eating all the silkworm cocoons because the cats were no longer keeping them under control. The emperor still wouldn't allow the cats to work, so the silk manufacturers placed statues of cats around the cocoons to scare the mice away. As you might imagine, this had no effect at all, and eventually the Emperor was obliged to put the cats back to work to save the silk industry.

In Tokyo, there is still an ancient temple dedicated to cats, called the temple of Gotokuji. This is not only a place of worship but also a necropolis for cats. Outside, people hang prayer boards for cats which are sick or have gone missing. The temple is protected by Maneki-neko, a Japanese folklore cat who represents the spirits of all the cats buried there. Her statues surround the altar, each with its right paw raised in greeting. These statues are often referred to as "beckoning cats."

right: **Prayer boards for sick or missing cats are hung outside the Inari shrine in Japan.**

above: **A statue of Maneki-neko, the friendly "beckoning cat" of Japanese folklore.**

left: **Cats were originally brought to Japan by Buddhist monks and are still regarded with deep respect.**

below: **Lucky charms and toys in the form of cats are very popular in Japan.**

Scandinavian myths

Freya and her cats

The Norse equivalent of Bastet—and Artemis and Diana—was Freya. She was the moon goddess, the goddess of fertility and all things feminine, and also goddess of death, especially of those killed in battle. Freya traveled in a chariot which was originally drawn by four lynx, but once the domestic cat reached northern Europe these were portrayed as cats. For a long time, people in Scandinavia used to put down four saucers of milk outside the door at night for Freya's cats.

When the witch-hunts first began in medieval times, the accused women were often forced to confess to night-time flights through the sky. These nocturnal journeys were often said to be led by Freya, carried in her chariot which was drawn by a group of cats. The Christians demonized Freya by portraying her as a witch and punished her cats by turning them into black horses. After working hard for seven years, however, the horses were allowed a reward: they were turned into witches… disguised as black cats!

Thor was challenged by a giant to perform several feats. One of these was to lift up an enormously large and heavy gray cat from the ground. Eventually, Thor succeeded in raising one of the cat's paws from the ground but he could not do no more.

The giant then told him that the cat was not really a cat at all, but the great serpent which encompasses Midgard (the Earth) in disguise.

below: **The goddess Freya's chariot was drawn by cats. Painting by N.J.O. Blommer, *Freja Seeking her Husband*, Nationalmuseum, Stockholm, Sweden.**

above: **The great sky god, Thor, who tried to lift a giant gray cat.**

Domestic cats, once introduced, were reckoned to be appropriate for Freya, the goddess of love, beauty, and all things feminine, since they were gentler than the wild lynx, and abundantly good breeders. It is interesting that, even before the cat reached Scandinavia, Freya was already associated with their nearest equivalent. The great god Odin gave Freya dominion over the "ninth world"—another connection between cats and the number nine.

Thor, the sky god

Cats made another appearance in Norse mythology, when the sky god Thor did battle with a huge cat in response to challenges from the giant Utgard-Loki.

This myth is yet another example of the link between the cat and the serpent, for the cat was the world serpent Jormungand in disguise, both representing eternity and, in this case, being almost interchangeable.

European myth and folklore

The cat found its way into Celtic lore as it did with so many other mythologies. It seems that the Celts were influenced by the Greek tales about Hecate, since their cat goddesses were dark and frightening characters.

One Celtic goddess, Danu, probably started out as a fertility goddess but evolved over time, eventually taking on a much more terrifying nature altogether. In the Dane hills in England's Leicestershire she became known as Black Annis. This witchlike woman often took the form of a cat and had enormous sharp teeth and long fierce nails or talons. She traveled only at night and fed on humans, preferably children. This particular habit is almost certainly an echo of the ancient Hebrew story of Lilith.

According to the Hebrew *Talmud*, Lilith was the first wife of Adam. But she disobeyed him and was punished by being expelled from Eden. She became an evil vampire who sucked the blood from newborn babies. She liked to disguise herself as a great black cat, known as El Broosha.

The Corn Cat

Europe has its own version of an agricultural deity who keeps the land fertile and protects the crops. Across the continent, this deity was worshipped as the Corn Cat. Unfortunately this frequently involved sacrificing cats, whose spirits were then released to look after the harvest.

In many parts of Europe, sacrificed cats were buried beneath fields and fruit trees to bless the harvest. The Corn

above: **Adam and Eve with Cain and Abel, engraved after the painting by Raphael.**
left: **There is a long association between cats and corn, due to the cat's link with fertility.**

Cat itself supposedly took refuge in a special sheaf of corn which was kept through the winter until the next spring's crops were sown for it to live amongst. This special corn sheaf was what is now known in England as a corn dolly, a symbol of a fruitful harvest.

The legend of the Corn Cat has given rise to many practices through the centuries, some of the less gruesome of which are still alive today in a few communities. In many places a cat was ritually sacrificed just as the last sheaf of grain was cut. Sometimes, the harvesters would all stand around the final sheaf and throw their scythes at it in turn to cut it, rather than having any one man held responsible for killing the Corn Cat. Today there are still places where people dress as cats at the end of the harvest or they decorate a live cat with ribbons.

Another Celtic cat goddess was the Scottish Cailleach Bheur, also known as the Blue Hag of Winter. She was a winter goddess who brought the snow and was born every year on October 31 (Samhain or Hallowe'en). Every spring she was finally defeated by the goddess Brigid who turned her to stone, on April 30 (Beltane or May Eve).

Cat superstitions

Cats are the subject of a huge range of superstitions, not least because they were demonized for so long in the West. Many of the superstitions about cats can be traced to beliefs or practices from the old mythologies. For example, the lion's association with water in ancient Greece—and therefore the cat's too—may account for its supposed ability to predict rain.

One of the oldest superstitions about cats which is still held to this day by some people is that you should never allow a cat to sleep alongside a baby, since it will suck the breath from the child and kill it. This superstition dates back to the ancient Hebrew story of Lilith taking the form of a cat and killing sleeping babies. There is, of course, no truth in this, as the Russians will testify: they held the opposite attitude that you should put a cat into a new cradle before the baby started using it because the cat would drive away any evil spirits.

The cat as cure-all

The cat was frequently seen as a kind of scapegoat (or scapecat) for illnesses. Many superstitions involve being able to transfer illnesses to a cat or cure them using cats. This kind of superstition may well be influenced by the ancient Egyptian view of Bastet as the great protector; the Egyptians often wore amulets in the shape of a cat's head to protect them from illness and evil.

According to one account from the middle of the eighteenth century, a woman whose hand was badly swollen transferred the complaint to a cat by holding her finger in the cat's ear. The pain had gone within a couple of hours but the unfortunate cat was in so much agony that it took two strong men to hold it down.

Cats could protect buildings as well as people, apparently. It was a practice until only a couple of hundred years ago to entomb a dead cat, sometimes with a dead rat as well, in the wall of a new house as it was being built. The purpose of this was to keep rats away from the building.

right: **Renior's *Mother and Child* shows a toddler petting a cat, an action considered dangerous in some cultures.**

below: **Dead cats and rats were often bricked up in the walls of new houses and barns, to protect people from live rats.**

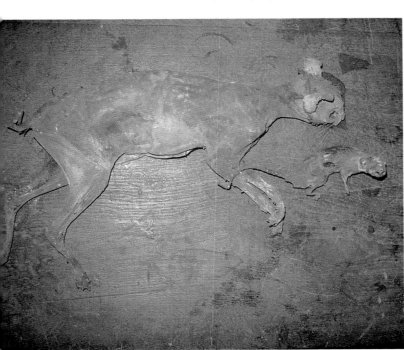

above: **Cats are reputed to know when a storm is on its way.**

right: **Frost is on the way, according to the position in which this cat is sitting.**

Cats and the weather

Cats are undoubtedly more sensitive to changes in the weather than humans. They often seem to know when a storm is coming, and there are even cases of cats moving their kittens out of the path of a tornado before it strikes. In rough weather, they often behave as if they "have the wind up their tail." All this has given cats a reputation for being associated with the weather in mysterious ways. During the medieval witch trials, cats were accused of controlling the weather, not simply responding to it.

There are all sorts of superstitious beliefs which involve being able to predict the weather from watching a cat's behavior. If the cat puts its paw behind its ear when washing, it means that it will rain soon—the gesture is sometimes known as "pulling down the rain." If it sits with its back facing the fire, it's a sign of frost. If it runs around

clawing at the furniture, expect a storm. And if the storm does hit, there used to be a belief in eastern Europe and in Scotland that you should throw the poor cat out of the house. Lightning bolts were apparently thrown by angels in order to drive evil spirits out of the cats; so keeping the cat indoors was inviting a lightning strike on your house.

Ships' cats

The cat's supposed affinity with the weather made it an important focus of superstition for sailors. After all, the more information they could glean about the weather, the better. In both Europe and Japan, cats were taken to sea in order to predict or even control the weather. A mewing cat signified a hard journey ahead and throwing a cat overboard was guaranteed to raise a storm. Shutting a cat up in a cupboard or in any other small space would raise the wind; sailors' wives would sometimes shut up their cats in order to keep their husbands at home.

In many places it was considered very unlucky to say the word "cat" on board a boat, even though it was considered lucky to have a cat on board. A black cat crossing your path on your way to the fishing boat is a very bad

above: **Scrumpy, mascot of the Royal Navy frigate HMS Sparrow, serving with the British Commonwealth fleet in 1953.**
below left: **Lucky or unlucky? It's a question of geography.**

sign, and you should simply turn round and go back home. If the catch is very bad, Scottish fishermen still sometimes say "We met the cat in the morning."

Lucky or unlucky?

Whether or not a cat, especially a black one, is lucky depends largely on where you live. In America, the first English settlers brought with them the attitude that a black cat crossing your path was bad luck, and this view still prevails. In England, however, such a meeting is considered good luck—as it is in Japan, where cats are generally considered beneficial. It is unlucky, however, if a black cat crosses in front of a woman on the way to her wedding, perhaps harking back to the ancient association between cats and fertility.

The whole month of May was considered unlucky by the Celts, since the first of May was sacred to their god of death. The Christians took over this view and May remained unlucky. As a result of this, kittens born during May were considered unlucky and were often killed; it was commonly thought that if they were allowed to live they would bring snakes into the house.

CHAPTER 5

above: **Hallowe'en wouldn't be the same without black cats, the witch's traditional companion.**

the cat
and
witchcraft

Cats and the Early Christians

Contrary to what you might think, the cat was once a sacred animal to Christians, though a relatively minor one, and many myths and tales surround it.

There is a folk tale that when Christ was born there was a cat in the stable giving birth to a litter of kittens at the same time. The Christ child wouldn't sleep, so His mother asked all the animals in the stable if they could help, but none of them was able to get Him to sleep. Finally, a little grey tabby kitten climbed into the manger and curled up next to Him, and He fell asleep to the gentle sound of its purring. The Madonna rewarded the kitten by allowing all tabby cats from that time forth to wear a letter M (for Madonna) on their foreheads.

It is an indication of the strength of later Christian feeling against cats that you will rarely, if ever, see a nativity scene with a cat in it to this day. But the early Christians had no such prejudice. Cats were introduced to Ireland in the fourth or fifth century AD by the monks, who used to include pictures of them in their illuminated manuscripts. The wonderful illuminated copy of the gospels, known as the *Book of Kells*, which dates from the eighth century, contains many pictures of cats. They tend to represent judgment and are often depicted with mice or rats who represent human souls. One Christian folk story tells how God created the cat in order to defeat the mouse which had been created by the devil.

The ancient influence

Cats were associated with some of the early Christian female saints. One of these was St Gertrude, to whom both the cat and the mouse were sacred. Another was

above: **When cats fell from grace, the black cat was the most vilified of all.**

left: **The "M" marking on the tabby's forehead has been attributed a sacred origin, associated with the Madonna.**

Details from the Irish *Book of Kells*, the manuscript of the four gospels, written in the eighth or ninth century:

right: **A cornerpiece showing two cats, with rats fighting over the communion water.**

below: **A pair of wrestling cats form an illuminated letter.**

St Agatha, who was often known as Santo Gato or Saint Cat. She was said to turn into a fierce cat when she was angered by women who worked on her feast day—a habit which is reminiscent of Sekhmet, the lion-headed, more ferocious face of Bastet.

Early Christian attitudes to cats seem to owe a great deal to more ancient cultures; just as the great fertility mother goddesses were always associated with cats, so too was the Virgin Mary. The Madonna and child were often depicted with a cat by artists such as Leonardo da Vinci.

And the festival of the Assumption, which celebrates the body and soul of the Virgin being taken into heaven, was set on August 15 by the early Christians—the day sacred to Artemis/Diana in pagan tradition.

Much of this positive view of cats was so well covered up by later Christians that many of us are still virtually unaware of it. It is all the more shocking, then, that the cat descended so swiftly into its association with witchcraft and devilry which lasted for around 500 years from about the thirteenth century.

above: **A 19th-century print of three witches with their cats.**

The cat's descent

So what happened to knock the cat off its pedestal? In the thirteenth century people were starting to become disillusioned with the Church and the structured society which it dominated. The Church needed to retaliate, and it needed a scapegoat on which to blame this unrest. It picked on witchcraft, perhaps partly because the main targets were weak, often old, women, who wouldn't make much of an opposition, and perhaps, too, because witches were a good focus around which everyone else would rally to the support of the Church.

One of the Church's great targets was women who belonged to the cult of Diana, which the Church claimed was a popular focus of worship for women. Some modern historians believe that this cult never existed at all, but certainly it was never of any significant size, and had nowhere near the number of followers the Church somehow unearthed.

Diana and her counterparts—Artemis, Freya, Bastet, and the rest of them—were obvious targets for many reasons. First they were female and associated with women because they were fertility goddesses. Second they were also associated with death and the underworld, and therefore with witchcraft. Diana's dark side was Hecate, an ancient goddess connected with the black arts, and Diana and her brother Lucifer had mated and their daughter was a teacher of witchcraft. Thus Diana was an obvious choice for the early Church to declare war on.

Tarred with the same brush

What about the cat? All these goddesses were symbolized by cats, and Diana was often depicted in classical art with a cat at her feet. Needless to say, this poor cat was transformed into her familiar, and the association between cats and witchcraft was born.

The Church had another argument against cats. They were mentioned only once in the Bible, and that was in the Apocrypha where they were referred to only in association with idols. It is likely that the Jews deliberately avoided any mention of anything sacred to the Egyptians who had governed them, but it gave the Church another weapon in its fight against the cat: it could not be accused of contradicting the Holy Bible in its campaign.

The cat, which had once symbolized the Virgin Mary's divine fertility, now came to represent treachery and stealth. It was no longer incorporated into paintings of the Madonna, but was associated instead with Judas. Paintings of the Last Supper often show a cat sitting at the

top: **Like witches, cats come into their own at night.**

left: **According to the medieval church, witches were as likely to fly on cats as on broomsticks.**

The cat as an agent of the devil

The new medieval Christian folklore adapted the old stories. Now, cats were invented by the devil. In fact, not only were they invented by him, they were often the devil in disguise. This did little for the status of cats, especially black ones, who were avoided studiously. In Slavonia, for example, the people would keep away from black cats at night because they believed that during the hours of darkness they had the ability to assume the form of the devil himself. In Ireland, a traditional greeting when entering a house was, "God save all here, except the cat." Cats became a common feature of rites to raise the devil.

In one Scottish ceremony it was necessary to throw a live cat backward into a kiln with two doors. The devil worshippers would all assume certain positions to invoke Satan. When he appeared, they would throw the cat in his face. This had the effect of obliging him to answer any question and grant any wish they made of him.

A seventeenth-century Danish woman gave birth to a child which had a deformity which gave its head an odd appearance. She was prosecuted for witchcraft on the grounds that the baby had the head of a kitten and she had therefore clearly been consorting with the devil.

below: **A witches' sabbath, by Gillot.**

above: **This is the form in which the devil was said to appear to the Knights Templar.**

Cats and Templars

The Knights Templar was an order of knights which was formed in the early twelfth century to give safe passage to pilgrims on their way to the Holy Land. To begin with the Templars were seen as brave and noble knights, prepared to risk their lives for the benefit of others. But as time went on, they began to accumulate wealth and power and became corrupted. They were mistrusted and disliked by the common people, and feared by rulers because they were so powerful. The Knights Templar was a very closed society, however, and therefore liable to accusations of secret practices. Eventually, the Inquisition was persuaded to accuse the Templars of heresy and, in an extraordinary raid on October 13, 1307, all the Knights Templar in France were arrested, tortured, and tried for heresy. Under

torture, many of them were forced to confess to worshipping the devil in the form of a black cat, sacrificing babies and young girls to him.

The Templars were not the only group accused of such practices. Many other religious sects, such as the Albigensians and Waldensians were also "persuaded" to confess to devil-worshipping ceremonies in which the devil appeared in the form of a black cat. One group, the Cathars, allegedly took their name from the fact that the devil appeared to them in the form of a cat. This was believed by many despite being transparently ridiculous—they didn't call themselves Cathars at all but Bons Hommes. (They had been christened Cathars after the Latin *cathari* meaning "the pure.")

The witch's familiar

For centuries, just owning a cat was considered incriminating evidence against anyone accused of witchcraft. As late as the nineteenth century one woman in the southeast of England was cast into a pit simply because she happened to own a black cat. One of the alleged associations between cats and witches was the belief that witches could turn themselves into cats. It was held that they sometimes employed this ability in order to fly through the sky on broomsticks, although sometimes they simply rode on the cat instead—harking back to the old stories of the goddess Freya being carried through the sky by cats.

Some people believed that a witch could turn herself into a cat nine times during the course of her life, and this gave rise to the saying (which still persists in some places)

that you should never speak ill of anyone in front of a cat. This makes sense according to the logic of the time because the cat might not be a cat at all, but a witch in disguise. One eighteenth-century account tells of a witch turning herself into a cat:

Not only could witches transform themselves into cats but, in some places, it was thought that cats could turn into witches. There was a belief in Hungary that most cats would turn into a witch after the age of seven. To prevent this, they cut the sign of the cross into the cat's skin.

Five hundred years of witchcraft

The trial of the Knights Templar in 1307 was the first major trial for witchcraft and atypical of later trials in that it was men, not women, who stood accused of having dealings with the devil. Although men were accused throughout this era of the witch hunts, it was women who were far more at risk of accusation from neighbors with a grudge or locals looking for an explanation for blighted crops, perhaps.

above: **Part of a woodcut depicting three witches and their cats, from a seventeeth century broadsheet reporting their trial.**

left: **Modern witches often keep and use cats. This is Cassandra Latham, the village witch of St. Burayn, Cornwall, England.**

In 1563, the English government passed an act of parliament against witchcraft, and the first trial took place two years later. The sixteenth and seventeenth centuries were the worst times for the persecution of both witches and cats, and the most feared figure of all was the Witchfinder General. He was a "pricker" of witches who extracted numerous confessions from both men and women. In particular, many of these confessions included admissions of owning or conversing with familiars, generally cats. (Familiars were an aspect of witchcraft confessions which was particularly British.)

below: **The Witch by Thoma (1870) depicts a stereotypical scene of the black cat in the witches den.**

Robert Tinbull was spelled on the bridge over an hour by Hester Dale, the old witch of Marrick. His horse would not move until Tom Wilson came along with a rowan staff. Then they both saw Hester run over the road as a black cat. They both knew it was her, because she had meant him harm for a good while.

above: **An engraving of Witchfinder General Rodgers catching a witch.**

The last witchcraft trial in England was in 1712, when a woman was found guilty of witchcraft on the sole grounds that she had conversed with the devil in the form of a cat. She was ultimately pardoned, however. In Europe witches were still being executed well into the mid-eighteenth century.

Famous witch trials

One of the most notorious witchcraft trials was held in 1582. This was known as the "trial of the St Osyth witches," and was the first time that a group of women was accused of operating as a coven of witches. Thirteen women from St Osyth in Essex, England, were tried, ten of them accused of killing people through witchcraft. They were also accused of the usual range of other crimes such as souring milk, causing the death of farm animals, and so on. Two of the witches were found guilty and hanged; one of them had been accused of possessing four spirits, two of them cats—one gray and one black. Two more of the accused were also said to have four imps, all of them "like unto black cats."

Another trial took place in 1596 which now appears ludicrous in light of the facts. It took place in Aberdeen in

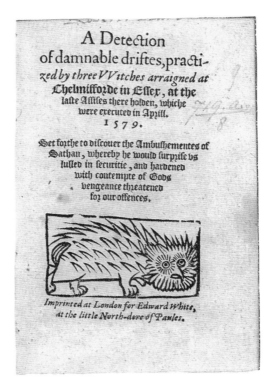

Scotland which was rife with accusations of witchcraft at the time. In this case, a group of women was accused of a number of offenses of witchcraft, including the allegation that they turned themselves into cats in order to hold orgies around the town's Fish Cross in the market square. It seems not to have occured to anybody—or if it did they didn't voice it—that the animals in question could have been real cats, attracted to the fish market by the smell. There was a spate of witchcraft trials in Aberdeen in 1596-7 as a result of which 24 people were burned.

above: **Title page of a book describing the Chelmsford witchcraft trials (1579). The animal illustrated is thought to be a cat.**

below: **A young woman accused of witchcraft by Puritan ministers appeals to Satan to save her.**

The plot against the king

The trial of the "North Berwick Witches" ran for two years, from 1590, and was the most notorious of all the Scottish trials. It all started because a town bailiff became suspicious about the night-time activities of one of his servant girls. He tortured her, and then handed her over to the authorities. She started to make all sorts of confessions under torture, which gradually became more and more convoluted, and dragged numerous other local people into the line of fire. The central confession, it emerged, was that a group of witches had been plotting to kill the Scottish king, James VI. Almost one hundred witches had supposedly decided to kill the king by raising a storm at sea to shipwreck and drown him and his queen, Anne of Denmark, as they returned to Scotland from Denmark. And how had they plotted to raise this storm? In the age-old way, it was alleged, using a cat. They supposedly baptized a cat, tied dead men's limbs to each of its paws, and then threw it into the sea thus summoning the power of the storm. It was said that James was only saved by his great faith in God.

right: **A cat or a witch? Not only was it believed that witches could turn into cats, but that cats could turn into witches.**

below: **King James was allegedly the target of a witchcraft plot.**

right: **Many women and men were burnt at the stake as witches, and their cats along with them.**

Witches as scapegoats

It was common practice to find explanations for natural calamities in witchcraft. Rather than accept that a cow had died of illness, for example, it was frequently assumed that it must have been bewitched. In the case of James VI and the storm, it was not enough that a storm had blown up naturally—it must have been caused by foul play.

Another pair of women, sisters Margaret and Philippa Fowler, were accused on this same principle. They were dismissed from the service of the Earl of Rutland, whose two children had died—almost certainly from a fever. However the women were blamed and forced to confess to having caused their deaths. Philippa admitted to taking a glove belonging to the little boy, Lord Henry Rosse, and giving it to her mother, who had then rubbed the glove against her cat, Rutterkin, then boiled it, and buried it. It was claimed the boy and his sister had died as a result. Margaret and Philippa were both executed for witchcraft (though strangely, the mother was not put to trial).

Not only black cats

Although owning a black cat was the most incriminating evidence against a woman accused of being a witch, the cat didn't even have to be black to be a liability. In 1565, a woman called Elizabeth Francis "confessed" that she had a white spotted cat, allegedly named Sathan, to whom she fed not only bread and milk but also her own blood. Elizabeth was accused of the most fantastical crimes—of employing the cat to kill a man who had got her pregnant and who then subsequently refused to marry her. The cat then told her how to abort the pregnancy. According to the prosecution, Elizabeth then passed this cat on to Agnes Waterhouse who turned it into a toad. This toad then proceeded to kill numerous livestock in the area. Both Elizabeth Francis and Agnes Waterhouse were hanged for witchcraft.

It was not only women who were accused of witchcraft. In Mora, Sweden, in 1699, three hundred children were tried. The charge against them was that they had used their cats to steal food for the devil. Fifteen boys were condemned to death, while 36 others were made to stand in the pillory every Sunday for a year.

above: **The black cat was officially damned by Pope Gregory IX, shown here, c.1230.**

The persecution of cats

The cats, of course, were not merely bystanders in the witch hunts. While the witches were being burnt or beheaded, the cats were being victimized too.

In fact, cats were being persecuted even before the witch trials began.

Pope Gregory IX officially announced the link between black cats and the devil in the tenth century, and in 962 hundreds of cats were burnt for their sins during Lent in the town of Metz, France.

During the Renaissance another pope, Innocent VIII, ordered the killing of every cat in Christendom. From this time on, cats were routinely killed until King Louis XIII of France put an end to the law—though not always the practice—at the beginning of the seventeenth century. Ironically, this history of persecution may well have had a detrimental effect on the spread of the Black Death, because as a result there were far fewer cats to kill the rats which carried the disease.

The burning of cats

Cats were generally killed by burning, often in wicker baskets suspended above bonfires. The idea of this was to prolong their suffering before death, and therefore make the devil suffer too. In some places fireworks were thrown into the fire along with the cats. The Celts had held a traditional midsummer fire festival at which sacred animals were burnt as sacrifices. The Christians superimposed St John's Day on this festival, and perpetuated the practice of burning animals, this time cats as creatures not of veneration but of evil.

The French, in particular, used to burn cats on the eve of St John's Day. One of the greatest followers of this practice was King Louis XIV. Reference to this custom is made in a surviving receipt from a certain Lucas Pommérieux for money paid to him for "furnishing for a period of years, ending with the feast of St John 1573, all the cats collected for the usual bonfire, and also for furnishing the large jute bags to carry the aforesaid cats."

above: **King Louis XIV of France, an enthusiastic burner of cats.**
below: **Cats were often suspended in wicker baskets over a bonfire to be killed.**

In 1558, after the accession of Queen Elizabeth I of England, the anti-Catholic crowds in London created huge effigies of the Pope from metal and straw, filled them with cats, and burned them. The Pope was considered the Antichrist, and the cats symbolized diabolic influence.

Cat fireworks were set off in Flanders. In 1582 a high-masted ship was set up in the market place at Bruges. It was filled with fireworks and then live cats were chained to it. When it was lit, the cries of the cats mingled with the bangs and crackles of the gunpowder and created a great display which apparently impressed the crowds.

Tortures galore

Burning was not the only method employed for killing cats. In certain places cats were thrown from towers. This practice was popular in Belgium, where it was used to signify a renunciation of the goddess Freya and her cult.

Other methods of cat torture included the cat organ. This grotesque piece of equipment was a keyboard which, instead of operating pipes or hammers like a traditional organ or piano, pulled the tails of cats which were trapped in cages. The tails were pulled hard enough to encourage the cat to emit a loud sound, to the apparent amusement of the onlookers. It was customary to release the cats from the organ, eventually, so that they could be used for target practice by archers. Not only archers, but also knights on horseback used live cats as targets. In Danish jousting tournaments the horsemen used their lances to impale barrels filled with cats.

The ability of the human imagination to dream up tortures for cats was, sadly, almost unbounded. People used to put cats in pots and then shoot at them. Or they would trap them in a barrel which was suspended on a rope between two posts and then throw cudgels at the barrel.

In northern Europe cats were often killed by being cudgeled to death.

In England, cats were often whipped to death, in the "game" known as "whipping the cat." When the River Thames in London froze over in winter, people would organize events and attractions on the ice. The signboard for these would sometimes consist of a caged cat on top of a post. When enough people had been attracted to the place, the cat would be shot to loud cheers of encouragement from the crowd.

below: **The cat organ, consisting of cats trapped in cages, was one of the most gruesome forms of cat torture.**

Cat throwing at Ypres

In the town of Ypres in Belgium, there was a long-standing tradition of throwing cats from the top of the Cloth Tower. This seems to have been started at least as early as the twelfth century and continued until 1817 when it was finally outlawed. Originally only one or two cats were thrown, but it became the practice to throw two cats in a bad year and three cats in a good year. Although not verified, this cat throwing is thought to have originated as a renunciation of heathenism and the worship of the goddess Freya.

The cat throwing tradition was outlawed in 1817 but was resumed in 1938 when velvet cats were thrown from the Cloth Tower instead of live ones. Since 1958 the festival, which was originally held during Lent, has been moved to the second Sunday in May. It is still held to this day, and is now a major festival and tourist attraction.

Today the history of cats and human culture in Ypres is celebrated in a procession which includes a statue of Bastet, the goddess Freya, seated 20 feet high drawn along by two cats, and a giant Knight Templar. After this a witch

above: **The Cloth Tower from which the "cats" are traditionally thrown.**

below: **A giant cat is paraded through the streets of Ypres.**

top and above: **Everyone takes part in the modern celebration of the cat.**

left: **A representation of the Cat Queen.**

trial that culminates in witches being burnt is depicted. The people of Ypres are dressed up as cats and appoint a Cat Queen. She and her jester then climb the Cloth Tower and the jester throws down velvet and fabric cats to the crowds below. It has been a long haul for the cat but today even Ypres, one of the centers of cat persecution during the witch hunt era, is able to celebrate the history of the cat with a festival in which cats are honored rather than harmed.

CHAPTER 6

above: *Child Posing with Cat*, a classic example of American folk art, attributed to Beardsley Limner.

the cat
in art and
literature

Early art and literature

The cat has been a popular subject for both artists and writers for thousands of years. The earliest examples of cats in art date back to Egyptian times, when they appeared in wall paintings, paintings on papyrus, on decorated pots and urns, and in sculpture. The Egyptians painted and sculpted real cats as well as representations of their cat-headed gods, especially Ra and Bastet.

left: **Egyptian temple wall relief, Dendara, Egypt.**

below: **This marble relief from Poulopoulos, near Athens, circa 510-500 BC, shows two people encouraging a fight between a dog and a cat.**

The ancient Greeks also depicted cats, although few examples survive. One that does is a scene at the base of a statue dating from the fifth century BC. It shows a group of men encouraging a cat and a dog to fight each other.

The Greeks also created the earliest literary cat. In the sixth century BC Aesop wrote his collection of fables, which include several cat stories. He depicts the cat as sly and wily and it is almost always the villain in the fable.

left and above
(from bottom left clockwise):

An Egyptian green faience figure of a cat crouching (seen side view and head-on); late Egyptian bronze of a cat with her kittens; large bronze head of a cat.

Christian art

As time moved on cats were incorporated more and more into art. In medieval times they appeared in the Irish *Book of Kells* and in other illuminated religious manuscripts such as the Lindisfarne gospel. The cat was presented in a good light in these representations and mostly was used to symbolize judgment.

Renaissance art was really the high point for cats in early art. One of the most enthusiastic cat painters was Leonardo da Vinci, whose drawings include a well-known page of sketches of cats. Some of these are extremely well

right: **Page and detail from the *Lindisfarne Gospels* written in AD 698 in the monastery at Lindisfarne, Northumberland, England. The cat is on the initial page of *Luke*, its hind legs and tail at the top, its elongated body, containing eight birds, running down the right-hand margin, and its front legs and head at the bottom.**

drawn, while others seem surprisingly ungainly. Cats frequently appeared in paintings of the Madonna and child as the Virgin Mary's symbol of fertility, and Antonello da Messina's famous painting of *St Jerome in His Study* shows a cat sitting at the feet of the saint.

The cat soon declined in reputation, however, and before long artists were using it to symbolize evil and treachery. Not only did a cat appear at Judas' feet in many depictions of the Last Supper, but it was also present in other scenes such as Tintoretto's *Annunciation* and Goya's *Ensayos*.

In the seventeenth century, Jean de la Fontaine wrote his fables which featured a cat by the name of Raminagrobis. This cat was similar in character to Aesop's, being wily and devious. In one fable, *The Cat, the Weasel, and the Rabbit*, the cat is asked to settle a quarrel between the other two characters. Pretending to be old and deaf, Raminagrobis asks them both to come close so he can hear their argument clearly. When they move nearer to him, he kills and eats them both.

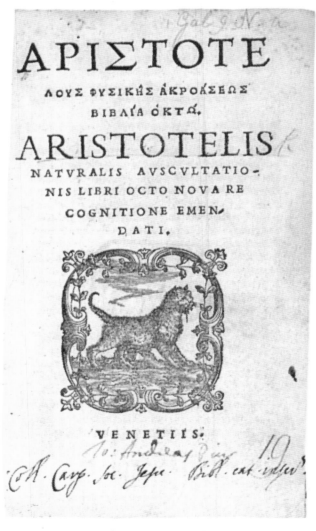

above: **Tintoretto's *Annunciation* with a cat on the lower left-hand side symbolizing evil.**

right: **An edition of Aristotle's works, showing a cat on the frontispiece, published in Venice in 1545.**

vs puſillu
nomen eſt q
hır. latınū
reſ quod ex humoꝛı
muſ ꞇra. unde & hu
mo ꞇeꞇur creſcıꞇ. ſıꞇ
augentur; que rurſuſ mınuente luna de
eſt eo qꝺ ꞇodaꞇ & ın modum ſerre preꞇ

Cats in art

After the Renaissance period when cats fared rather badly in religious art, the situation improved for them. Some seventeenth-century painters often included a cat in portraits; the cat usually looked extremely relaxed and was often sitting beside the fire. By the eighteenth century cats were generally painted as themselves, rather than as some symbol of devilry or treachery. From then on, cats became a regular feature in all forms of art. So much so, that even George Stubbs, the English painter who specialized in paintings of horses, included a cat in *The Godolphin Arabian*. This late eighteenth-century painting was made 40 years after the horse's death; the cat was included to illustrate an anecdote about it. The cat had shared the horse's stable with it and, when the horse died, the cat kept a vigil beside its body. When the body was taken away the cat slunk off to the hayloft and died shortly afterward.

In the eighteenth-century folk painting below, there are still overtones of the old symbolism of cats; an atmosphere of decadence is suggested by the abundance of wine glasses and the poses of the figures. The giant cat

above: **Henry Wriothesley, 3rd Earl of Southampton, painted with his cat by John de Critz the Elder in 1603. Reproduced by kind permission of His Grace, the Duke of Buccleuch, from his collection at Boughton House, Northamptonshire.**
below: **Eighteenth century painting (American) depicting a cat under the table.**

above: *Le Chat Noir* is one of Steinlen's most famous cat paintings.

above: **Kuniyoshi, woodblock print, *Girl chastising a thieving cat*, c.1845.**

top and above: **Louis Wain specialized in humorous paintings of anthropomorphized cats. Here we see a cat family looking for lodgings and cats bathing from bathing huts.**

that lurks beneath the table clutching a dead mouse is perhaps hinting at the licentious undertones of this festive scene.

Cats were a popular theme with late nineteenth-century French artists, especially Théophile Steinlen, whose beautiful cat drawings and paintings still appear on postcards today. Steinlen drew thousands of cats, mostly based on the local cats he saw wandering the alleys near his house, which became known as "Cat's Corner." Edouard Manet also painted many cats, as did his friend Auguste Renoir, one of whose most famous paintings is

Girl with a Cat. Although she was English, the artist Gwen John (1876–1939) spent most of her life in France where she lived with several cats. She painted many fine portraits of cats which have increased in value since her death.

The most popular Victorian cat artist was undoubtedly Louis Wain, who painted many entertaining pictures of cats pursuing very human activities such as tea parties or breakfasts. Wain gave an insight into his technique when he wrote: "In drawing my cats, I always commence by drawing the ears first; *in every case I do this,* and if I try any other way the proportions are certain to go wrong." Wain's cats were in many ways the forerunners of many other twentieth-century cartoon cats both drawn and animated, from Felix to Garfield, taking in many popular favorites such as Tom of the duo Tom and Jerry, Sylvester, and Top Cat, to name just a few.

Cats have long been popular subjects for art in the East as well as the West, especially in Japan where artists have produced many beautiful paintings of cats. Some cat paintings, often on silk, date back centuries. Many of the later ones depict the Japanese Bobtail cat—the Japanese breed with a distinctive short tail which dates back to the early part of the nineteenth century.

right: **Daisey the college cat at St. Catharine's College, Cambridge, England, showing that cats, too, appreciate art.**
far right: **Edouard Manet, *A Woman with a Cat* c.1882 (Tate Gallery, London).**
below: ***My Wife's Lovers*, the largest and most valuable American antique painting of cats. It was painted in 1891 by Carl Kahler for Mrs. Kate Birdsall Johnson of San Francisco. It now hangs on exhibit at Kaja Veilleux Antiques in Newcastle, Maine.**

Cats in American folk art

Folk art is generally regarded as being the art of the common people; it is separated from the fine art produced by trained and professional artists. Most folk artists were probably tradespeople or craftspeople who worked in a field related to art, so they had some basic training or skills in a relevant field. One of the effects of this is that many of the paintings, although lacking the studied techniques of the professional fine artist, have a quality that is spontaneous and fresh.

America has a strong tradition of folk art, most of which dates from the eighteenth century onward. It is a particularly interesting form of art from the point of view of the social history it documents. The subject matter illustrates the fashions, styles, and costumes and gives a clear picture of the lifestyles, interests, and preoccupations of the people of the time.

Many examples of American folk art depict cats, often with children, and almost always giving a view of cats as well-loved family pets. Some artists have chosen to paint a portrait of the cat itself, while others simply include cats in family portraits or scenes of home life. Either way, the cat comes across as an integral part of American family life over the last few hundred years.

top: **A mid-19th-century portrait of a cat family at play,** *Cats and Kittens*, **artist unknown.**

above: **In this portrait of Mary Jane Smith, by Joseph Whiting Stock, Springfield, Massachusetts, 1838, the child points at her playful cat.**

above: **In this colorful painting, *The Quilting Party*, a cat is threatened by a dog as part of a thriving domestic scene.**

above: **A cat plays under the table in this picture of a family at home, attributed to Joseph H. Davis.**

Patres noftri in egypto non in
tellexerunt mirabilia tua: non fue
runt memores multitudinis mife
ricordie tue
Et irritauerunt ascendentes in

Cats in literature

Since the times of fables and fairy tales, cats have continued to feature widely in literature. Some of these stories feature cats in an affectionate, companionable light, while others show the darker side of the animal, harking back to many of its earlier associations. One example is in Edgar Allen Poe's _The Black Cat_. Despite the nature of this fearsome cat, Poe was actually a cat lover, and had a favorite tortoiseshell called Catarina.

Other literary cat lovers have included the Brontë sisters, Mark Twain, Harriet Beecher Stowe, Ernest Hemingway, and Henry James. Charles Dickens also owned a cat which was called "The Master's Cat," who used to distract him from his writing by snuffing out candles with its paw.

left: **Mid-19th century portrait of _Mrs. Josiah B. Keylor's Cat_, artist unknown.**

Poetic cats

Let take a cat, and foster him well with milk
And tender flesh, and make his couch of silk,
And let him see a mouse go by the wall
Anon he waiveth milk and flesh and all
And every dainty that is in that house,
Such appetite has he to eat a mouse.

These lines come from Chaucer's _Manciple's Tale_, demonstrating—if demonstration were needed—that cat behavior hasn't changed since the fourteenth century. Cats have been featured by noted poets down the centuries, including Shelley and Keats, two leading poets of the Romantic Era.

Edward Lear owned a cat called Foss for 17 years, who was part of the inspiration for many of the cats in his nonsense verse. The most famous of these must be the beautiful cat in *The Owl and the Pussy-cat*.

One of the cat lover's favorite poets must be T.S. Eliot, whose *Old Possum's Book of Practical Cats* was published in 1939. He owned many cats, and his poems grew out of years of making up cat poems for children. His book contains poems about over a dozen cats, all of them unique and delightful, ranging from *Macavity, The Mystery Cat* to *Skimbleshanks: The Railway Cat*. The musical *Cats* is based on the book and is a celebration of feline mystery and grace.

left: **One of Nicolas Bentley's characterful illustrations from T.S. Eliot's *Old Possum's Book of Practical Cats*.**

above and below: **T.S. Eliot's *Old Possum's Book of Practical Cats* was adapted into a highly successful musical.**

above: **Illustrations of his own cat, Foss, by Edward Lear (1812–88).**

above: **Some of Edward Lear's illustrations for his poem** *The Owl and the Pussycat* **(1871).**

Library cats

One of the more recent societies to be formed in the USA is the Library Cat Society (LCS) which was founded in 1987. This organization promotes the establishment of cats in libraries, whether as a form of rodent control or simply for PR purposes. It has members across the country, and many of the libraries it is associated with have well-known cats of their own.

The most famous of these were undoubtedly Baker and Taylor, two Scottish Fold cats who lived in a library in Minden, Nevada. They were the mascots of the company Baker & Taylor, the world's largest distributor of books to libraries and bookstores. Another cat promoted by the LCS is Muffin, who was evicted from a library in Puttnam Valley, New York, because one of the library's

trustees became allergic to cats. Two local residents were so disheartened by the eviction that they deleted the library from their wills, costing it $80,000 in legacies.

top: **Cats, with their reputation for wisdom and intelligence, seem natural inhabitants of libraries.**

below: **Melville Dewey of Eastham Public Library, Eastham, Massachusetts, guards the book drop.**

clockwise from top left: **Baker and Taylor, late of Douglas County Public Library, Minden, Nevada. Carnegie of Rochester Public Library, Rochester, New Hampshire. Libby keeping watch over the books at Haysville Community Library, Haysville, Kansas. Pointing the way at the University of Cambridge, Cambridge, England. Monty, the resident cat at Montgomery Elementary School Library, Farmers Branch, Texas**

Cats in children's literature

Cats appear particularly often in children's books. There seems to be an affinity between cats and children, and certainly many cat stories are extremely popular with children. Today's favorites include *Nicky's Noisy Night* by Harriet Ziefest, and the *Tenth Good Thing about Barney*, by Judith Viorst. In the nineteenth century, Lewis Carroll's *Alice's Adventures in Wonderland* centered around a little girl called Alice who owned a cat called Dinah. In the course of the book, she also meets the grinning Cheshire cat, who explains to her why he is completely mad. When the Cheshire cat has finished talking to Alice he disappears slowly and the last thing to vanish is his enormous grin.

By the time Carroll wrote the sequel, *Through the Looking Glass*, Dinah—who featured once again—had produced two kittens as well, named Kitty and Snowdrop.

At the very beginning of the twentieth century, Rudyard Kipling brought out a collection of stories which he had originally made up for his children, under the title *Just So Stories*. One of these magical tales was the story of *The Cat that Walked by Himself*, which relates Kipling's version of the domestication of various animals and their relationships with people. It tells how the Man and the Woman tamed the Dog, the Horse, and the Cow, but never quite mastered the Cat: "He will kill mice, and he will be kind to Babies … but between times, and when the moon gets up and the night comes, he is the Cat that walks by himself, and all places are alike to him."

Beatrix Potter included cats in several of her children's stories. Many of these were set in the Lake District in northwest England, where she spent the later part of her life, and featured scenes and characters from her own life. It is very likely that Tom Kitten and his sisters, Moppet and Mittens, along with their mother Mrs Tabitha Twitchit, were based on real cats that Beatrix Potter either lived with or knew well.

Cat illustrators not surprisingly model their creations on their own cats if they can. Another popular children's cat is Orlando, the Marmalade Cat, who appeared in nearly 20 books between 1938 and 1972. He was created by Kathleen Hale, whose beautiful drawings were based on her own cats. It is impossible to list every cat that

PIG AND PEPPER. 91

"Well, then," the Cat went on, "you see a dog growls when it's angry, and wags its tail when it's pleased. Now *I* growl when I'm pleased, and wag my tail when I'm angry. Therefore I'm mad."

"*I* call it purring, not growling," said Alice.

"Call it what you like," said the Cat. "Do you play croquet with the Queen to-day?"

left: **Rudyard Kipling's own illustration for The Cat that Walked by Himself from the Just So Stories.**

far left: **The grinning Cheshire Cat from Alice's Adventures in Wonderland by Lewis Carroll, illustrated by Sir John Tenniel.**

appears in children's literature, because there are so many, from Paul Gallico's cats Jennie and Thomasina through William Mayne's Calico Cat.

Perhaps one of the first that young children come across is *The Cat in the Hat*. This wonderfully subversive and humorous character was created by Dr Seuss in 1957 as the first in a series of reading books for beginners. And what story could be better for a child learning to read than a tale about a cat?

right: **Tom Kitten having his buttons sewn back on, illustrated by his creator Beatrix Potter.**

below: **Orlando the Marmalade Cat in *A Trip Abroad* by Kathleen Hale, 1939.**

Cats in nursery rhymes

Cats frequently appear in children's nursery rhymes and have done for centuries. Some are apparently nonsense verse, while others are used to teach children skills such as the ABCs.

> *Great A, little a, bouncing B,*
> *The cat's in the cupboard*
> *and she can't see me.*

Several nursery rhymes refer to a cat with a fiddle, such as *Hey Diddle Diddle, the Cat and the Fiddle*, and this seems to be a reference to the sistrum, a four-stringed musical instrument of the Egyptians, which was one of Bastet's emblems. Another example of this kind of rhyme, which is first recorded in 1740, strengthens this connection by featuring a female cat.

> *A cat came fiddling out of a barn*
> *With a pair of bagpipes under her arm;*
> *She could sing nothing*
> *but Fiddle cum fee*
> *The mouse has married*
> *the bumble bee.*
> *Pipe cat, dance mouse;*
> *We'll have a wedding at our goodhouse.*

This rhyme supposedly refers to a real incident during the time of Queen Elizabeth I. One of the best-known accumulative rhymes dates from a little later, about 1750:

> *This is the cat*
> *That killed the rat*
> *That ate the malt*
> *That lay in the house that Jack built.*

The rhyme *Ding dong Bell, Pussy's in the Well* is at least four hundred years old and is mentioned several times by Shakespeare in his plays. Dating from around the same period is the rhyme:

> *Pussy cat, pussy cat,*
> *where have you been?*
> *I've been up to London*
> *to visit the queen.*

right: **Cat by Edward Topsell from *The Historie of Foure-Footed Beasts* describing the true and lively Figure of every Beast...,1607.**

above: **The cat and the fiddle is a popular image dating back to the goddess Bastet.**

below: ***The Cat in the Hat* is one of the classic creations of modern children's literature.**

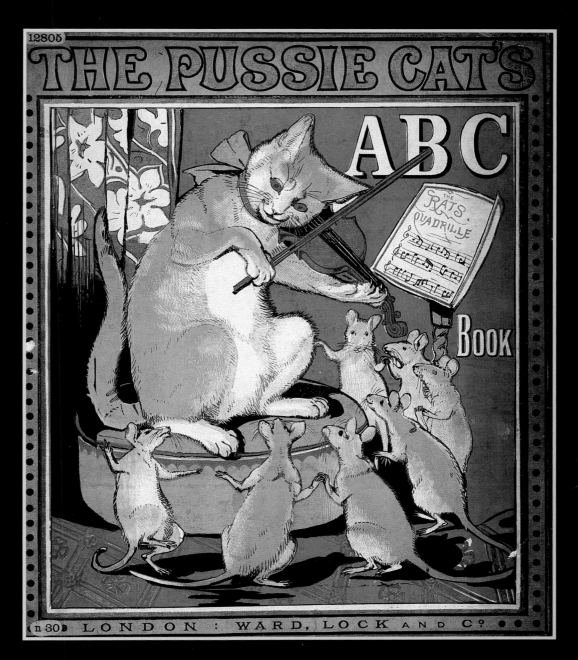

above: *Pussie Cat's ABC book*, Artist unknown, 1880.

below: **Two highly collectable picture books; *The Playtime Book* published by Ernest Nisler, illustrated by Helena Maguire (early 20th century) and *With Louis Wain in Pussyland* published by Raphael Tuck around 1910–1920.**

above: **Dick Whittington and his cat, engraved from the original of le Brun.**

Dick Whittington and his cat

Around the seventeenth century many fairy tales became popular, several of which featured cats. One of these stories was the tale of Dick Whittington and his cat. It was even older, dating back to the fourteenth or fifteenth century.

According to this story, Dick Whittington grew up orphaned and very poor in a little country village in England. He decided that his only hope of a better life was to go to London where the streets were said to be paved with gold. However when he arrived, he found things were just as bad as they had been in the country. He found very little work, he was lonely, and he was nearly starving.

One day, despairing and exhausted through hunger, he collapsed on the steps of a smart town house.

The owner was a wealthy merchant, Mr Fitzwilliam, who felt sorry for Dick and offered him a job in the kitchen. Dick was treated terribly by the cook but the family were kind. He had his own little attic room to sleep in but unfortunately it was plagued by rats and mice. One day a visitor to the house gave him a penny for cleaning his boots, so Dick set off to the market where be bought a cat. He was very fond of her and she kept his little room free of rats and mice. Soon, one of Mr Fitzwilliam's trading ships was due to sail for the Barbary Coast. It was the habit for everyone in the household to send something to trade. Dick had only his cat so he sent her, although he was very sorry to part with her.

top: **Dick sends his cat to trade on Mr. Fitzwilliam's ship, artist unknown, 1845, and** above: **Dick's cat sets off for the Barbary Coast, artist unknown, 1845.**

above: **The memorial to Dick's cat stands on the spot where Dick Whittington turned back, on Highgate Hill, North London, England.**

As time went on, Dick became increasingly tired of being treated badly by the cook and eventually decided to run away. He left early one morning but as he reached Highgate Hill he heard the bells of Bow ring, and they seemed to be saying "Turn again, Whittington, thrice Mayor of London." He was so encouraged by this prophecy that he returned home.

Soon the trading ship returned and it transpired that the King of Barbary had been so impressed with the cat that he had bought her for ten times the value of everything else on the vessel. He had been plagued with rats and had never seen a cat before. Mr Fitzwilliam was a fair man, and insisted on giving the entire fortune to Dick, refusing even to keep a share. Dick was suddenly a wealthy man and then went on to become a rich trader himself.

He rose to become Lord Mayor of London three times, just as the bells of Bow church had predicted.

It is true that London did have a Lord Mayor by the name of Sir Richard Whittington, who held the post three times, although there is no evidence that he ever had a cat. Some people think the story derives from his having a type of trading boat known as a cat. But stories about people who succeed as a result of being kind to cats were very popular at the time, *Puss-in-Boots* being another well-known example.

These tales may well have originated with the "matagot," a magician cat whom the people of southern France and other places believed in. It was thought that a matagot would always bring good luck to anyone who treated it with kindness.

above: **The cat's senses are acute. It is highly attuned to what is happening in the world around it, and as such has gained a reputation for having a "sixth sense."**

the cat's
sixth
sense

The cat as Seer

The cat's ability to sense things that humans cannot is well documented as far back as ancient times. The ancient Egyptian word for cat was *mau*. This may simply have been the noise it made, but the word actually means "to see" or "to foretell," and it may have been given to the cat in recognition of its undoubted abilities as a seer.

above: **Mount Vesuvius, Italy. One couple were saved by their cat's warning when the volcano erupted in 1944.**

Sensing danger

As we saw earlier, cats seem to be extremely sensitive to changes in the weather. But this is not their only unusual ability. They are extremely sensitive to both vibrations and electrostatic activity in the atmosphere, and this seems to explain their extraordinary ability to predict dangers such as earthquakes, volcanic eruptions, and wartime air raids. This skill is well known among many people who live on the slopes of active volcanoes; in many parts of the world cats are kept as pets precisely so they can warn their owners of imminent eruptions.

left: **Cats can seem all-knowing, and many cat owners have no difficulty believing that their pets have a sixth sense.**
below: **Strange, fretful, or anxious behavior in a cat can be an indicator of an impending natural disaster.**

Cats as quake predictors

Cats can often predict earthquakes as well as volcanos. Chinese scientists have used this ability to their advantage in predicting major quakes. In 1975 seismologists evacuated the city of Haicheng just 24 hours before a major earthquake. Much of the information on which they had based their prediction of this earthquake came not from scientific equipment but from watching the behavior of certain animals, including cats.

One very well-documented example of this concerns a cat called Toto. This cat lived with his owners close to Mount Vesuvius in Italy. One night in 1944, Toto's owner was awoken in the middle of the night by his cat scratching him repeatedly on the cheek. He was angry with the cat, but couldn't get him to stop. Eventually, his wife decided that Toto was behaving so strangely because he sensed that the volcano was about to erupt. She persuaded her husband to get up, pack a bag quickly, and leave the area. An hour later their house was buried in molten lava as Vesuvius erupted, killing nearly 30 people.

In northeastern Italy in 1976, in the Friuli district, cats all over the area began to behave strangely. From early evening, many of the local cats were racing around wildly, scratching at doors, and disappearing as soon as they were able to escape. At nine in the evening, a major earthquake hit the area. This account is similar to accounts of cat behavior all over the world in regions affected by earthquakes, where often many of the local cats will sense that there is danger on the way.

Second sight

You may or may not believe in ghosts, but cats certainly seem to possess a sixth sense which enables them to see things we may be unable to see ourselves. This sixth sense appears to have been observed for thousands of years, since many ancient writings and practices associate cats with the gift of second sight.

The Hebrew *Talmud* contains instructions for seeing into the spirit world which involves putting powder in the eyes which is obtained by burning a black cat to ashes. And in parts of the Gold Coast of West Africa, the shamans wear cat skins around their necks to help them make contact with the spirit world. The ancient Britons, too, believed that staring into the eyes of a wildcat helped you see into the world of the spirits. And the eighth-century monk the Venerable Bede wrote of a gruesome ritual in Scotland in which cats were sacrificed. The cats were supposed to help raise the Black Cat Spirits, which would confer the gift of second sight.

Seeing ghosts

There are numerous accounts of cats apparently seeing the spirit or ghost of someone who has died. One of these is

above and below: Seeing things that we can't see? Not only are there many tales of cats who come back as ghosts, but living cats are also credited with an uncanny ability to see ghosts.

interesting because the cat in question seemed to see the ghost of another cat. A cat called Fingal had died and each evening his owner continued to hear a gentle tapping on the window at the time when Fingal had always tapped at the window to be let in after going out for the evening. One day a friend came to visit in the afternoon, bringing

her Siamese cat with her. The Siamese walked over toward the chair where Fingal always used to sleep in the afternoons. Suddenly it stopped, arched its back, and began spitting—just as though there was another cat already on the chair. After a while Fingal's owner happened to open the French windows, at just about the same time she always used to let Fingal out. As soon as she had done so, the Siamese got up and went straight over to Fingal's chair and curled up on it, exactly as though the chair had just been vacated.

Another famous story of a cat exhibiting strange powers concerned a cat called Fidget, whose owner was killed after being knocked down by a car. Fidget and his owner had been extremely close and, before he died, the owner had asked the hospital staff to arrange for a neighbor to look after Fidget. Two days after his death, the owner was buried in a nearby cemetery, and the brief ceremony was attended by the neighbor. The neighbor, however, was amazed to find when he arrived that Fidget was patiently waiting beside the empty grave. After the coffin had been lowered into it, the cat turned and walked slowly back home.

above: **The flexible backbone of the cat helps it to climb, and domestic cats will climb as readily as their wild relatives, indoors and out.**

below: **Cats can wait patiently in the same spot for hours.**

SYDNEY IS AT YOUR FEET

above: **Cats have been known to overcome huge obstructions in their determination to reach their destination.**

Psi-trailing

Cats have an extraordinary ability to find their way home over improbably long distances—the world record is a staggering 1,500 miles. This uncanny skill seems to have been recognized for thousands of years; there is an ancient Hebrew folk tale that tells how, when all the animals were expelled from the Garden of Eden along with Adam and Eve, the cat was only one that was able to memorize the route. As a result, cats still know how to find their way back to heaven.

It seems that cats have a similar ability to homing pigeons, for example, in possessing some sort of built-in navigational system. This may also combine with a strong territorial instinct which draws them back to their home. What is harder to understand, however, is the ability of some cats to turn up at their owners' new home after being left behind when the owners moved house.

Take the case of Rusty, a cat whose owners left him in Boston, Massachusetts, when they moved in 1949. Rusty arrived 83 days later on the doorstep of their new home in Chicago, Illinois, 950 miles away. This would have taken an average of over 11 miles a day, which almost certainly involved hitching lifts on cars or trains. To date, this is still the fastest average traveling speed of any cat when psi-trailing—the term given to this kind of navigating in animals.

Mistaken identity?

Sceptics quite understandably argue that identification of cats is so impossible that the owners may believe what they want to when a stray looking like their old pet turns up at the door. This is, of course, a fair point. And that's why a pair of researchers at Duke University, North Carolina, decided to conduct research into the subject which would rule out misidentification as an option.

The researchers publicized the fact that they were looking for cases of animals which had apparently traveled huge distances to be reunited with their owners. They received hundreds of responses but only selected about 50 for further investigation, on the basis of very strict criteria. First, they would accept only first-hand accounts from owners. Next, they needed independent eye-witness corroboration. Then they needed the animal to be alive so that they could examine it, and finally they insisted that it should have some kind of distinctive feature so that the identification could be guaranteed to be accurate.

below and right: **Numerous verified cases exist of cats traveling long distances alone, crossing roads, railroads, and rivers, and even hitching rides.**

The two researchers ended up with 22 cases of cat psi-trailing which met their stringent criteria. One example was a four-year-old cat who followed his owners almost 300 miles across Louisiana in 1954 when they moved house. He turned up at the school where the son of the family, whose cat he was, was a pupil. The cat ran away from the other pupils, but immediately allowed his owner to pick him up. This particular cat had been raised by the family dog, and had learnt to growl and bite when angry, and to answer to a whistle; the dog welcomed her as soon as she reappeared. It also had a distinctive scar over one eye which meant that it couldn't completely close it, and two other distinctive marks. This kind of evidence makes it hard to argue that this was not the same cat which had been left behind four months earlier.

Telepathic cats

Certain cats exhibit an uncanny talent for such close understanding with their owners that they appear to have some kind of telepathic link with them. They are able, somehow, to tune into the mind of their owner; in virtually all cases of this the bond between cat and owner is very strong.

Cat lover Ernest Bozzano recorded a strange telepathic link with his cat. On one occasion, he was busy writing late into the evening when he was suddenly overcome by a conviction that his cat needed him. He was so disturbed by this that he immediately went in search of her. She was nowhere to be found in the house, so he called for her around the garden. Eventually he heard a faint mewing in response, and tracked her down under a hedge, caught in a rabbit trap. The slipknot of the trap was around her neck and if she had struggled she would have been killed. Perhaps she recognized that her best chance was to communicate mentally with her owner to seek his help.

On another occasion, the cat was lost and the family searched the house and garden looking for her. Then suddenly Bozzano had a strong mental picture of a tiny room in the attic which was almost always kept closed. He went straight there and found his cat inexplicably shut in there. She seemed to have sent him a mental picture in order to help him to find her.

Perfect timing

Another example of strange telepathic ability in cats is some kind of sixth sense for judging time. One of the best documented instances of this is a cat named Mysouff, who belonged to the French writer Alexandre Dumas. When-ever Dumas came home from work in the evening, Mysouff would always arrive at the end of the street to meet him at the same moment that Dumas himself arrived.

What makes this particularly surprising is that Dumas usually returned at a regular time but occasionally he would be late home. His mother always opened the door for the cat at the same time but, on the days when Dumas was delayed, the cat would not jump down from his cushion and would refuse to move. Finally he would stir, leave the house, and reach the end of the street just as Dumas arrived there.

above: **Some cats are reputed to be able to send telepathic messages to their owners when they are trapped in a room or stuck up a tree.**

below and right: **In many cases cats will follow their owners a certain way down the street, or wait to meet them on their return. Dumas's cat would actually meet him at the end of his street each evening.**

above: **A family of pedigree Abyssinian kittens.**

breeding cats

Why people breed cats

Many people choose to keep a cat for companionship and aren't concerned whether it is a pedigree breed or not. In fact many people find the non-pedigree 'moggie' has a temperament which they prefer; certainly they are generally healthier and longer-lived. But for many other people, the cat is such a beautiful creature that they derive enormous pleasure from owning, breeding, and showing their favorite pedigrees.

above left: **A fine pair of Korat kittens, and** above right: **Silver tabby Chinchilla Persian male cat "Cosmos."**

Cat breeding is a demanding occupation, and the standards set for pedigree breeds are extremely stringent. If a kitten is born with the wrong color eyes, or faulty markings on its coat, its value is diminished and it is no good for showing. Since people began to take pedigree cat breeding seriously, in the latter part of the nineteenth century, dozens of new breeds have been developed, some by fluke and others through generations of careful crossbreeding. Each show cat has to have the right eye shape and color, the correct shape of head, the right coat and markings, and the correct body shape to have any chance of succeeding at a cat show.

Setting standards

Every pedigree breed of cat has a breed number and a breed standard which stipulates the points on which cats of that breed will be judged. Many breeds are subdivided into varieties, which are different acceptable colors within the same breed. In the USA there are nine official associations, of which the most prominent is probably the Cat Fanciers' Association (CFA); in Britain, the breed standards are set by the Governing Council of the Cat Fancy (GCCF). The American and British standards for breeds are not identical; they vary in such factors as which coat colors are acceptable.

In the USA, all but a half dozen longhaired breeds are classified as "Persians," whereas the British system classifies each breed separately according to coat length—long or short. The British also divide all breeds into either British or foreign, whereas in the United States some specific breeds are classified outside these two divisions.

The genetics of breeding

Cat breeding requires a detailed understanding of genetics, particularly since mating two different cats together can often throw up a range of coats and patterns which neither parent necessarily exhibits. Some genes are sex-linked, which means they will only show up in one or other sex. The gene for tortoiseshell cats, for example, can only produce female tortoiseshells.

Some breeds cannot always breed true, because a kitten which inherited two genes for a particular trait would die in the womb; so any live cat must carry only one gene for the particular trait instead of two. This applies to the Manx gene which produces a cat with no tail, for example, and to the Scottish Fold gene, which produces a cat with "folded" ears.

below: **Cream and white Manx.**

Symbolizing genes

As in the human, genes in the domestic cat exist in pairs—one received from each parent—for each feature. The genes for each feature are either dominant or recessive to its opposite feature. For example the normal "wild-type" coat of the *Felis catus* is shorthaired, and is symbolized, for convenience sake, as *L*. The opposing genetic feature to short-hair (*L*) is long-hair, which is recessive to short-hair and is symbolized *l*. Dominant genes are symbolized with an upper case letter, and their corresponding recessive gene with the lower case version of the same letter.

Sperm and ova contain one of each pair of the parents' genes, so it may be seen that some features are passed on in a fairly random fashion. Once the dominance or recessivity of the genes is understood, however, it is fairly simple to deduce methods of manipulating the genes by careful selection of breeding partners in order to produce offspring with the desired traits.

A simple example is the production of long-hair in cats, as demonstrated in these charts.

1 A homozygous shorthaired female is mated to a homozygous longhaired male (*LL* x *ll*).

2 A heterozygous shorthaired female is mated to a heterozygous shorthaired male (*Ll* x *Ll*).

3 A heterozygous shorthaired female is mated to a homozygous longhaired male (*Ll* x *ll*).

KEY

♂ⓘ	**gene from male**
♀Ⓛ	**gene from female**
L	**short-hair**
l	**long-hair**

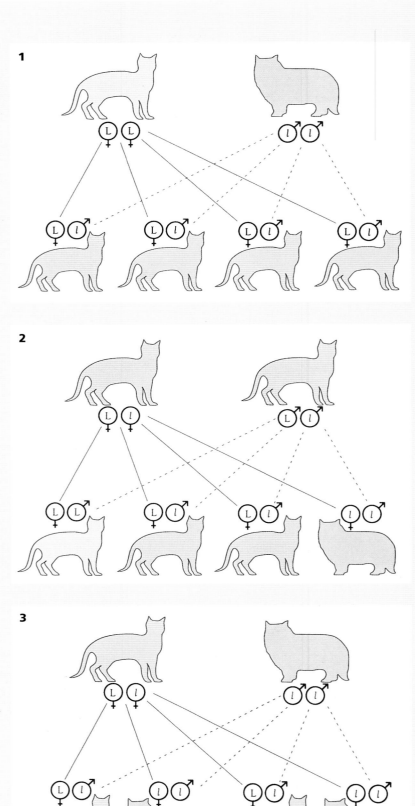

Standards

It's hardly suprising that there are so many recognized varieties of cats, when you consider the number of variables there are. Their eye color, eye shape, coat colors, and coat markings all give breeders the opportunity to breed a wide range of very different-looking cats (as well as some varieties which are perhaps less distinct to the untrained eye).

Cats' eyes

A cat's eyes can be one of three basic shapes: round, almond-shaped, or slanted. The shape of the eyes varies according to the breed, orientals tending to have slanted eyes for example. There are six basic eye colors: orange or copper, yellow, hazel, and green being the first four. The two remaining colors are different shades of blue; dark blue is generally found in Siamese cats, while pale blue is characteristic of white cats. This is the same pale blue eye gene which is often associated with deafness.

The cat's coat

When it comes to the coat, there are nine basic colors which can, of course, be overlaid with other markings. These are black, chestnut brown (US) or chocolate (UK), caramel brown (US) or cinnamon (UK), blue, lavender (US) or lilac (UK), light lavender (US) or light lilac (UK), red, cream, and white. There are some other minor colors which are sometimes classified as basic colors, such as the cream Burmese, which occurs only in Burmese cats.

Once again, certain colors are related to certain breeds —the British Blue is always blue, for example—although many breeds can exhibit a variety of colors. In a large number of breeds, the basic coat color is overlaid with a pattern of some sort.

eyes **Different breeds of cat have distinctively different eye shapes.**

Round

Longhaired or Persian cats as well as most of the shorthairs have large, round, eyes.

Oval/Round

Some breed standards call for oval or almond-shaped eyes often tilted at the outer edge towards the ears.

Oriental

Siamese and similar related breeds have eyes of Oriental shape, set slanting towards the outer edge of the ear.

solids **Cats of self- or solid-colored breeds must be of a single, solid color throughout with no patterns, shading, ticking or other variation in color. These are the most common solid colors.**

Black	Blue	Chocolate	Lilac
Red	Cream	Cinnamon	White

Coat patterns

Patterns can occur in a range of colors or color combinations. There are four varieties of tabby patterns; ticked, mackerel, spotted, and classic. These varieties can come in a wide range of colors, of which we show only a selection.

Mackerel refers to finer dark stripes, and ticked fur looks like hare or rabbit fur. It can also be found in the Abyssinian and other cats bred originally using the Abyssinian. Each long guard hair has bands of different colors in it, giving a more gently shaded version of the classic ticked look. Shaded and tipped patterns appear when the tip of each long guard hair is a different color than the rest of the coat. Both can occur in a wide color range, and on short or longhaired cats.

The Himalayan coat pattern, or colorpoint, is found in cats such as Siamese, which have a single coat color all over except at the "points," in other words the nose, ears, feet, and tail. Sometimes a solid second color appears on the points, but it is quite possible to have tabby points too. Tonkinese cats show a modified "pointed" effect.

Tortoiseshell, or multiple coloring is exclusive to female cats (and a few sterile males as a result of chromosome abnormality). It is generally a mixture of black and orange markings, with the orange markings showing a tabby pattern. However, it is possible to have tortoiseshell markings in other colors, such as lavender and cream.

Piebald coat patterns contain spots or blotches of white, which can cover anything from just the nose, feet, or bib of the cat to almost the entire coat.

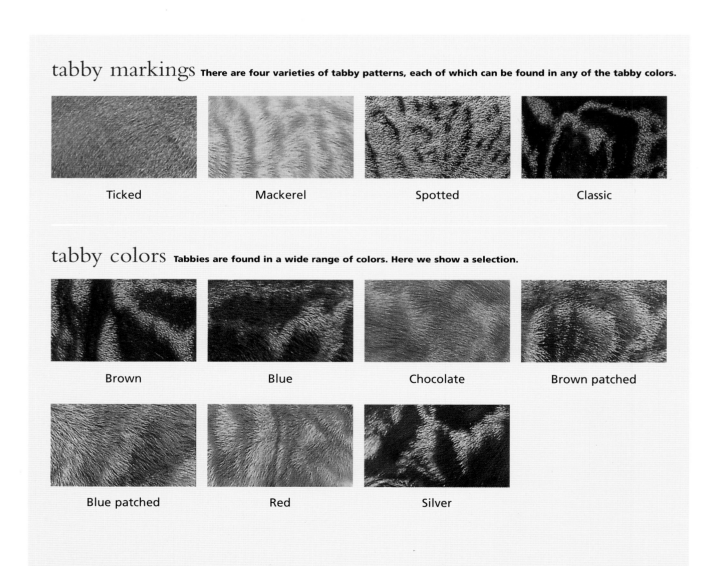

tabby markings There are four varieties of tabby patterns, each of which can be found in any of the tabby colors.

| Ticked | Mackerel | Spotted | Classic |

tabby colors Tabbies are found in a wide range of colors. Here we show a selection.

| Brown | Blue | Chocolate | Brown patched |

| Blue patched | Red | Silver |

abyssinian
Abyssinian cats have coats which are gently shaded, because each hair is lighter at the root and darker at the tip.

Usual

Blue

Sorrel

Fawn

colored tips
Coats of this sort, with the hairs darkening in various degrees towards the roots, are found in a number of colors, some of which are shown here.

Black smoke

Blue smoke

Chocolate smoke

Lilac smoke

Chinchilla silver

Chinchilla golden

Black tipped silver

Blue tipped silver

himalayan
Cats with the Himalayan coat pattern, such as the Siamese, have pale coats with the main color restricted to the head and extremities.

Seal point

Blue point

Red point

Cream point

Lilac point

Chocolate point

Seal point

Red tabby point

tonkinese

Tonkinese cats, which are light-phase Burmese cats, show a modified "pointed" effect. The coats are darker than those of cats with true Himalayan coloring, so the "points" are not so dramatic.

Brown	Lilac	Chocolate	Red

Cream	Lilac tortie	Blue tortie	Tabby

multiple colors

As every cat lover knows, cats come in coats of many colors apart from those already described, most of which are recognized for show purposes in one breed or another. The tortoiseshells are the most common, but there are endless varieties, including the unusual Mi—ke pattern of the Japanese Bostail.

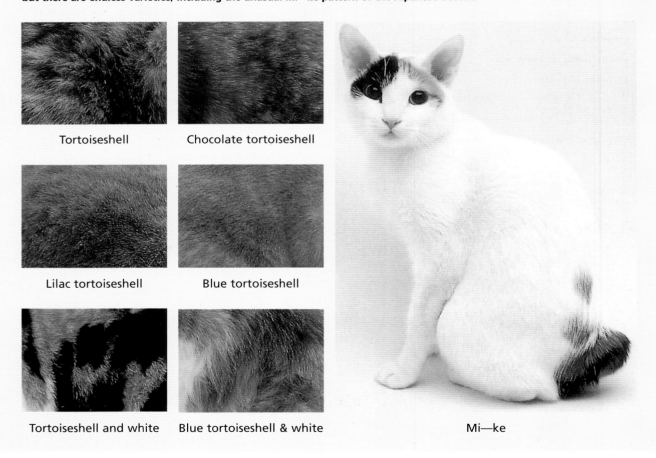

Tortoiseshell	Chocolate tortoiseshell

Lilac tortoiseshell	Blue tortoiseshell

Tortoiseshell and white	Blue tortoiseshell & white

Mi—ke

The ideal cat

There are two criteria on which a show judge will judge a cat: its general appearance and condition, and how closely it meets the breed standard. Each feature of the cat can attract a maximum number of points; together these points add up to 100. In some associations, particularly in the USA, the judge will write down the specific number of points awarded for each feature. In other associations the judge will make a general assessment, using the points system as a guide only.

There are certain features which result in points being deducted, which are specified in the breed standard, and certain features which disqualify a cat from competing, such as polydactyly, a condition which gives cats extra toes.

Head

In the US the head can attract 30 points including the size and shape of the eyes; in the UK 25 points.

This part of the standard covers the size and shape of the head, the ears and how they are set, the nose, and the cheeks. In the USA the size and shape of the eyes is also taken into consideration in this category.

Eyes

In the USA this is worth just 10 points because size and shape are categorized with the head; in the UK up to 15 points.

The size, shape, color, and spacing of the eyes is important for high scoring in this feature.

breakdown of 100 Show Points

NB Note different points scale in UK from USA.

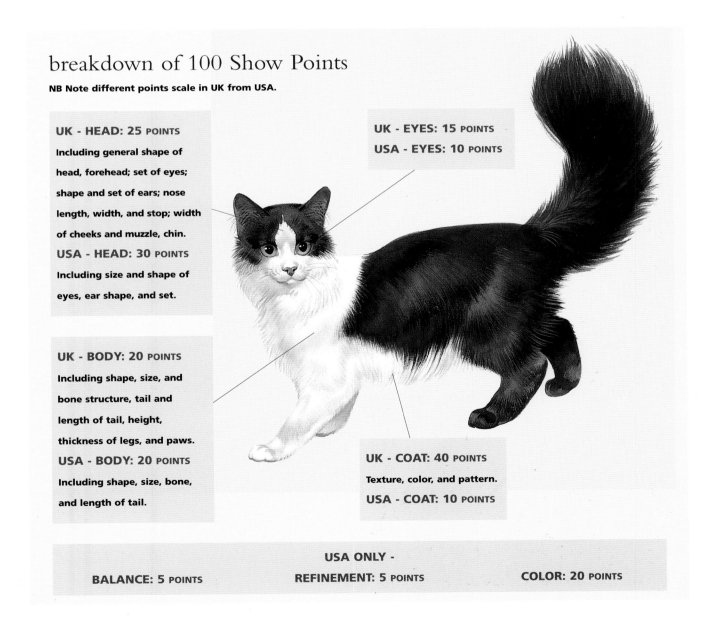

UK - HEAD: 25 POINTS

Including general shape of head, forehead; set of eyes; shape and set of ears; nose length, width, and stop; width of cheeks and muzzle, chin.

USA - HEAD: 30 POINTS

Including size and shape of eyes, ear shape, and set.

UK - BODY: 20 POINTS

Including shape, size, and bone structure, tail and length of tail, height, thickness of legs, and paws.

USA - BODY: 20 POINTS

Including shape, size, bone, and length of tail.

UK - EYES: 15 POINTS

USA - EYES: 10 POINTS

UK - COAT: 40 POINTS

Texture, color, and pattern.

USA - COAT: 10 POINTS

USA ONLY -

BALANCE: 5 POINTS   **REFINEMENT: 5 POINTS**   **COLOR: 20 POINTS**

Body

In the USA this is covered by the "type;" it is worth a maximum of 20 points and includes the tail; in the UK this counts for 20 points also.

This part of the judging considers the general build of the cat, and the length, straightness, and sturdiness of its legs. It will also take into account how deep the chest should be, and how level the back. The paws are judged in this section as well, looking at their shape and structure. In the USA the tail is also considered here: its length, how it is carried, and at what angle to the body.

Coat

In the USA this counts for 10 points and the color is judged separately; in the UK, 40 points including the coloring.

The length of the coat is obviously important here, and the judge will also look closely at the denseness and condition of the fur, and any tufts on the ears or toes. In the USA, neither the tail nor the color is included here, which explains the relatively low number of points this section carries. The color of the coat and how it meets the breed standard is judged in the UK, and the length, coat, and angle of the tail are also covered in this section in the UK.

Color

Only in the USA, this is worth up to 20 points.

The coat color is specified in the standard here, as well as the color of the lips, chin, nose, and paw pads.

top: **Friendly seal mitted ragdoll.**

above: **Two shorthair tortoiseshell kittens.**

left: **British shorthair kittens, silver spotted and smoke—10 weeks old.**

left: **A striking tabby shorthair.**

below: **Blue Burmese mother cat suckling two-day-old kittens (three brown, two blue).**

bottom: **Three white chinchillas—true "glamor pusses."**

above: **Red tabby Persian male cat among fall foliage.**

cat
breeds

Longhaired breeds
Persian

Before cat shows were ever thought of, the Persian, or longhair as it is known as in Britain, was a popular breed and recognized as a distinctive and separate form of cat. They first arrived in Europe during the sixteenth century and quickly overtook the already popular Angora.

The Persian is a large cat of some substance with a flowing and very full coat of very dense long fur. The body is sturdy and, apart from the legs, should be completely concealed by the fur. The head is large and round, as are the eyes. The ears are small. The fur around the neck forms a ruff and is longer than the body fur, and the long fur on the tail is extra bushy and resembles a fox's brush. Their overall build is medium to large, with massive shoulders and a muscular back. They have a very broad skull with full cheeks and powerful jaws.

The Persian cat's temperament is very easy-going, almost to the point of being placid. They are gentle cats and extremely playful. They make quiet but affectionate pets and are easy to have around the home.

The difference between American Persians and British longhairs, apart from the name, is that there are some colors not recognized in the UK, such as the brown patched, the blue patched, and the silver patched. Their selective breeding standards over many years have led to very pure characteristics in all the differing colors but they should all conform to the basic standard for the breed generally. For instance they can be penalized, no matter what color, if they carry a kinked or curved tail, have any apparent weakness in the hindquarters, or an asymmetrical appearance to the head.

Black Persian

Countries of origin: northern Asia, Turkey, Persia (now Iran)

Type:
cobby with short, thick legs;
round head with short nose;
large eyes

Facial characteristics:
round face; nose short;
eyes large and round,
copper colored or
deep orange

Coat:
long silky fur with soft underfur;
longer guard hairs; plumed tail

Color:
black

Temperament:
placid, friendly,
affectionate, gentle

Associated breeds:
Exotic shorthairs; other Persians

The Black Persian, or Black longhair as it is known in the UK, is a very large cat indeed with dense coal-black fur which should have no white hair at all; nor should it have any tinge, shading, or marking of rust or brown at all.

The Black Persian is one of the oldest breeds in pedigree form and also one of the most difficult to breed to top show condition. The black hair is very prone to developing brown markings which may be caused by damp conditions or strong sunlight. During their molt periods they also develop brown bars.

Young Black Persians may appear to be mismarked at first because they have lots of brown or rust-colored shading in their undercoat and their top coat seems pale and not a proper black at all. However these defects usually disappear as the cat reaches maturity.

A true Black Persian in tip-top show condition is a very handsome cat indeed with its glossy black coat and large orange eyes.

Blue Persian

Countries of origin: northern Asia, Turkey, Persia (now Iran)

Type:
cobby with short, thick legs; round head with short nose; large eyes

Facial characteristics:
round face; nose short; eyes large and round, copper colored or deep orange

Coat:
long silky fur with soft underfur; longer guard hairs; plumed tail

Color:
any shade of blue as long as it is uniform and unmarked

Temperament:
placid, friendly, affectionate, gentle

Associated breeds:
Exotic shorthairs; other Persians, including blue smoke Persian

For a Blue Persian, or Blue longhair as it is known in the UK, to be a true top show cat it must have a uniform overall hue. Any shade of blue is permitted as long as it isn't shaded or marked, and it mustn't have any white hairs. In the USA lighter shades are preferred while in the UK darker ones seem to be more popular. The eyes must be copper colored.

The breed is very old and the Blue Persian Society was formed in 1901. An early fan of the Blue Persian was Queen Victoria who may well have contributed significantly to their popularity which has remained up to the present time.

Faults in the Blue Persian include tabby markings and white on the chest although most blue kittens are born with tabby markings but they will disappear as the cat matures. Nose leather and paw pads should all be blue.

Chestnut Brown Persian

Countries of origin: northern Asia, Turkey, Persia (now Iran)

Type:
cobby with short, thick legs; round head with short nose; large eyes

Facial characteristics:
round face; nose short; eyes large and round, orange or copper

Coat:
rich medium to dark chestnut brown with similarly dark underfur

Color:
chestnut brown

Temperament:
same as Persian but more vigorous like the Siamese

Associated breeds:
other Persians

To produce a true Chestnut Brown Persian took quite some doing. First of all the colorpoint had to be developed—this is a Persian with distinctive Siamese markings.

This was done during the 1920s by mating Persians with Siamese. Once the colorpoint chestnut brown color was successfully transferred to the Persian, the breeding program for true chestnut browns could be developed. This didn't take place until the late 1940s when the first Chestnut Brown Persians were bred, almost by accident. Pure chestnut browns were found in litters of chestnut brown colorpoints. The first ones had a color that tended to fade easily and had weak eye colors.

All these problems have now been successfully overcome and the pure-bred Chestnut Brown Persian (or longhair in the UK) is a successful and popular breed as it combines the gentleness of the Persian with the enthusiasm of the Siamese.

Cream Persian

Countries of origin: northern Asia, Turkey, Persia (now Iran)

Type:
cobby with short, thick legs; round head with short nose; large eyes

Facial characteristics:
round face showing only the cream color; nose short; eyes large and round, rich copper

Coat:
dense and silky as per all Persians but with an overall color of rich cream

Color:
cream

Temperament:
even-tempered and gentle

Associated breeds:
other Persians

In the UK during the early part of the twentieth century Red Persians (or longhairs in the UK) were known as "Oranges." When the first Cream Persians started to appear in litters they were regarded as substandard, and were called "spoiled oranges," and were not regarded favorably. In the USA, however, the potential was soon spotted and the breed was established in its own right. The Cream Persian is a magnificently creamy cat, described as being the color of Devonshire cream. In the USA the color has to be "buff" while in the UK a range of colors is permitted from pale honey through buttermilk to a rich brownish cream. In any case they should have pink paw pads and a pink nose pad, and the fur color should be true right down to the roots.

The breed doesn't produce large litters so the cat is something of a rarity though it is still very popular.

Lavender Persian

Countries of origin: northern Asia, Turkey, Persia (now Iran)

Like the Chestnut Brown Persian the Lavender Persian had to wait to enter the world stage until the successful crossmating of Persians for their body characteristics and Siamese for their colorpoints. Once the chestnut brown had been stabilized in the late 1940s, it was quite an easy matter to extend to the Lavender Persian.

The true Lavender Persian is a stunning cat, with silky lush fur of a wonderful dove-gray-pink-lavender color. The color should remain true right down to the roots and there shouldn't be any shading, striping, or white hairs.

The paw pads and nose pad should be pink and the eye color is deep copper in the USA and a pale orange in the UK.

Type:
cobby with short, thick legs; round head with short nose; large eyes

Facial characteristics:
round face showing only lavender color; nose short; eyes large and round, rich copper eye color (or pale orange in the UK)

Coat:
full, flowing coat of dove-gray-pink-lavender

Color:
lavender

Temperament:
even-tempered and gentle

Associated breeds:
Kashmir, other Persians

Red Self Persian

Countries of origin: northern Asia, Turkey, Persia (now Iran)

"Self" means an overall color completely free of ghostly tabby markings. It is in itself a difficult task to achieve but combine it with producing a rich red color and you have an extremely rare cat indeed. Not that the Red Self Persian is a new breed—far from it. As early as 1895 these cats were being shown at the Crystal Palace shows in London, England, where they were known as Orange Persians. Only a year previously they were being exhibited as Red Tabby Persians and it seems that the breakthrough occurred around that time to get rid of the unwanted ghostly tabby markings.

By 1912 there were two distinct breeds—the Red Self and the Red Tabby—and both could produce true color litters. The red color has got progressively stronger and has gone from a warm rich orange to the deep red we know today. The red color should be strong throughout the coat with no ticking, striping, tabby marking, or shading. Nose leather and paw pads should be brick red and the eye color copper.

Type:
cobby with short, thick legs; round head with short nose; large eyes

Facial characteristics:
round face showing only red color; nose short; eyes large and round, and copper

Coat:
a deep rich red with no markings

Color:
red

Temperament:
gentle and affectionate

Associated breeds:
other Persians

White Persian

Countries of origin: northern Asia, Turkey, Persia (now Iran)

Type:
cobby with short, thick legs; round head with short nose; large eyes

Facial characteristics:
head broad and round with pink nose pad; blue or orange or odd-eye color

Coat:
long, silky, very fine

Color:
white

Temperament:
gentle, affectionate

Associated breeds:
other Persians

right: **White Blue-eyed Persian.**

below: **White Odd-eyed Persian.**

below right: **White Orange-eyed Persian.**

Most varieties of cat breeds are distinguished by different color coats, so what do you do with a pure white cat? There can be only one variety—the white sort. Nevertheless the White Persian has several varieties and it all depends on eye color, not fur color. There is the blue eyed; the orange eyed (known as the copper in the UK); and the odd eyed which has one blue and one orange eye. The blue-eyed White Persian is genetically predisposed to deafness and in odd–eyed whites this deafness will show on the side of the one blue eye. The White Persian is quite an old breed, being well established in Victorian times, but it was not officially shown at cat shows until 1903 when it was well received and immediately became immensely popular. This is the classic "salon" cat which rarely goes outside and is very much an indoor cat. It has a gentle nature and spends a long time grooming itself. You may have to help every day, though, as the fur is very prone to matting.

Bicolor Persian

Countries of origin: northern Asia, Turkey, Persia (now Iran)

Type:
cobby with short, thick legs;
round head with short nose;
large eyes

Facial characteristics:
round face showing both colors;
nose short; eyes large and round,
copper colored or deep orange

Coat:
long fur with soft underfur;
longer guard hairs; plumed tail

Color:
red and white, blue and white,
black and white, cream and
white, chestnut brown and white,
lavender and white

Temperament:
placid, friendly, affectionate,
and gentle

Associated breeds:
Exotic shorthairs; other Persians
and longhairs

top: **Red and white Bicolor Persian.**

right: **Black and white Bicolor Persian.**

The original bicolors were only black and white and were known as Magpies. However it was so difficult to maintain the breed standard that other colors were allowed—and the distinctive marking of the Magpie was broadened to permit a much larger range of colors and patterns.

The bicolors can be any solid color with white, such as blue and white, cream and white, and red and white. In the USA they should have white legs and paws as well as white on the chest and a white inverted "V" on the face. In the UK there isn't such a tight color definition and they can have colored legs and paws, as long as between a half and two thirds of the coat is colored.

Like all Persian cats, the bicolors need daily grooming with both a comb and brush, and they can do with frequent bathing to keep their fur oil free as excess oil can build up quickly.

Blue-cream Persian

Countries of origin: northern Asia, Turkey, Persia (now Iran)

Type:
cobby with short, thick legs;
round head with short nose;
large eyes

Facial characteristics:
round face showing both colors;
nose short; eyes large and round,
copper colored or deep orange

Coat:
long silky fur with soft underfur;
longer guard hairs; plumed tail

Color:
blue-cream

Temperament:
placid, friendly,
affectionate, gentle

Associated breeds:
Exotic shorthairs; other Persians
including blue-cream smoke

Although reports of early Blue-cream Persians appeared as long ago as the end of the nineteenth century, the breed wasn't officially recognized until 1930. The blue-cream coloring is actually a pale version of the tortoiseshell. The tortoiseshell has red and black patches, and the blue is dilute black and the cream a form of dilute red.

Early cat-lovers understood little of feline genetics. However, some, by careful observation, were able to deduce some of the results to be expected by cross-matings. Thus it took some time for the breed to get established owing to the fact that the coloring was "sex-linked," that is it was passed down the female line and it took quite a while before male cats would take the coloring and the breed could then be mated like-to-like.

In the USA the Blue-cream Persian has to have a blue coat with clearly defined patches of solid cream while in the UK the shades of blue and cream can be much more intermingled and with softer defining lines between the two colors. There are no show rules about a facial cream marking although a cream blaze is desirable. Eye color should be copper in the USA and copper or brilliant orange in the UK. There shouldn't be any green rim to the eye in either case.

Cameo Persian

Countries of origin: northern Asia, Turkey, Persia (now Iran)

Type:
cobby with short, thick legs;
round head with short nose;
large eyes

Facial characteristics:
round face showing both colors;
nose short; eyes large and round,
rose- or red-colored rims with a
brilliant copper eye color

Coat:
white undercoat with a mantle of
color tipping and clearly defined
patches on the face, sides,
and back

Color:
red, cream, blue, white

Temperament:
placid, friendly,
affectionate, gentle

Associated breeds:
Exotic shorthairs;
other Persians

The Cameo Persian, or Cameo longhair as it is known in the UK, was originally bred in the USA in 1954 as a result of matings between Smoke and Tortoiseshell cats. They are born almost white and develop the muted and subtle coloring as they mature. The fur is described as "sparkling" or "marbled," and was originally a pink hue but has now been developed to take in pretty well the whole possible range of fur color. The eye color should be a brilliant copper with a red or rose rim.

There are three distinct types of Cameo Persian—Shell, Shaded, and Smoke—to differentiate between the differing hues. Shell Cameos are very pale, Shaded Cameos a little darker, and Smoke Cameos the darkest of all.

Chinchilla Persian

Countries of origin: northern Asia, Turkey, Persia (now Iran)

Type:
cobby with short, thick legs; round head with short nose; large eyes

Facial characteristics:
round face; nose short; eyes large and round, emerald or blue-green

Coat:
pure white undercoat with hairs on the back, flanks, head, ears, and tail being tipped to give a sparkling appearance

Color:
cream, silver, pewter, gray, blue, gold

Temperament:
placid, friendly, affectionate, gentle

Associated breeds:
Exotic shorthairs; other Persians including Masked Silver Persian

For such a delicate cat the Chinchilla certainly has a long and glorious history. Early examples were being written about and recorded as long ago as 1893 when it was described as "a peculiar but beautiful variety." Chinchillas were exhibited at the first Crystal Palace cat shows in London, England, as Silver Grays and Chinchilla tabbies.

The very first Chinchillas were much darker than those we would expect to see today and were the result of matings between silver tabbies and other Persians of darker colors. The darker cats today are known as Shaded Silvers and Shaded Goldens, and the light ones are regarded as true Chinchillas.

Eye colors were at first allowable in a wide range from green through orange to blue. Today the only eye colors really acceptable are green or blue-green. The kittens are born quite dark and often with tabby markings; the coat should lighten and the tabby markings disappear as the cat matures.

right: **Chinchilla Golden Persian.**

Shaded Silver Persian

Countries of origin: northern Asia, Turkey, Persia (now Iran)

Type:
cobby with short, thick legs; round head with short nose; large eyes

Facial characteristics:
round face showing both colors; nose short; eyes large and round, green or blue-green (orange or copper in the UK)

Coat:
long, full, silky, white undercoat with black-tipped pewter color mantle

Color:
basic white coat with subtle black shading over the face, head, flanks, back, legs, and tail

Temperament:
gentle, very affectionate

Associated breeds:
other Persians

In the UK the Shaded Silver Persian is known as the Pewter Longhair. It is a remarkably beautiful cat, with a white undercoat and a mantle of black-tipped shading on the face, flanks, and tail. The coat runs from white on the chin to a quite dark pewter color on the back. Its chest, stomach, and under the tail should all be white as well. The legs should be the same color as the face. Generally the Shaded Silver Persian is very similar to the Chinchilla but darker.

The lips, eyes, and nose should all be rimmed with a thin line of black. The leather on the nose and paws should be a darkish brick red. In the USA the cat has green or blue-green eyes, but in the UK, the eye color is orange or copper with a black rim. The guard hairs should be delicately tipped with black rather than heavily colored and there should be a full neck ruff that grows down into a deep frill between the front legs.

Smoke Persian

Countries of origin: northern Asia, Turkey, Persia (now Iran)

Type:
cobby with short, thick legs; round head with short nose; large eyes

Facial characteristics:
round face showing only permitted color; nose short; eyes large and round, and copper colored

Coat:
long, silky

Color:
black, red, blue, cream, lavender

Temperament:
gentle, affectionate

Associated breeds:
other Persians

right: **Chestnut Brown Smoke Persian.**

below: **Red Smoke Persian.**

This is another very old long-established breed although you'd expect it to be a modern product of successful breeding. The first Smoke Persians were being exhibited at cat shows in 1893 but the breed remained extremely rare. Its success even today is down to one person—Mrs H V James—who produced the very first cat which she described as being somewhat disappointing because it was a deep cinder color rather than the blue she was expecting. She went on to breed the Smoke Persian successfully. Originally it was only black in color, but the overall effect was one of a smoky shading to the head, back, and flanks, with a white underbelly which only shows when the cat is in motion.

Today smokes come in many colors such as the blue, the red, the lavender, and the cream. Depending on the overall color, the paw pads and nose leather vary. For instance in the red smoke they should be rose, as should the eye rims, whereas the blue smoke has blue pads and rims, and the black smoke has black leather and rims. In all smoke cats the eye color should be a deep copper.

Tabby Persian

Countries of origin: northern Asia, Turkey, Persia (now Iran)

Type:
cobby with short, thick legs; round head with short nose; large eyes

Facial characteristics:
round broad head with small ears; large round eyes (copper or hazel depending on color type); deep rose pink nose leather; tabby markings in an "M" on the forehead

Coat:
long, silky, tabby marked

Color:
in the USA red, brown, silver, blue, cream, cameo, patched, chestnut brown, lavender; in the UK silver, red, brown

Temperament:
gentle, affectionate, the tabby may well be more independent than other Persians

Associated breeds:
other Persians

The Tabby Persian has been responsible for far more arguments and bitter controversies in the cat world than probably any other cat. These have included quarrels about color, markings, and eye color. And these arguments continue to this day. In the USA almost any color is acceptable, from silver to tortie, brown to red, and cream to cameo; but in the UK only three varieties are permitted—silver, red, and brown. The tabby markings, now generally divided into two camps, are known as the classic and the mackerel. The classic has broad tabby markings with a clearly defined "M" on the face, a ringed tail, and rings of tabby rather than lines.

The mackerel, on the other hand, has much thinner tabby markings with lines rather than rings and the tail is barred rather than ringed. In the USA some colors, such as the chestnut brown tabby and the patched, are allowed a hazel eye color, but in the UK only a copper eye color is allowed.

above: **Brown Tabby Persian.**

right: **Lilac Tabby Persian.**

Tortoiseshell Persian

Countries of origin: northern Asia, Turkey, Persia (now Iran)

Type:
cobby with short, thick legs; round head with short nose; large eyes

Facial characteristics:
head broad and round with pink or black nose pad; copper eye color

Coat:
basic black with red and cream patches

Color:
tortoiseshell

Temperament:
gentle, affectionate

Associated breeds:
other Persians

Although the Tortoiseshell Persian has been around since the late nineteenth century it still remains one of the most difficult cats to breed, simply because the litters are always virtually all female. Male Tortoiseshell Persians are extremely rare indeed, and are always sterile. The breeding program in the USA seems to have been more successful than in the UK where true tortoiseshell Persians (or longhairs as they call them) are still very rare.

To produce a successful show cat you need a basic black cat with unbrindled patches of red and cream. You also need the cat to have a red or cream, or both, blaze running from the forehead down onto the nose. The pads should be pink or black; the nose leather pink or black; the fur color should be black, red, and cream, and evenly distributed over the entire body. Obviously producing a cat with all this is extremely hard; and it must also adhere to the basic cobby Persian shape and have the same gentle temperament.

Calico Persian

Countries of origin: northern Asia, Turkey, Persia (now Iran)

A recent introduction to the cat world, the Calico Persian is known as the tortoiseshell-and-white longhair in the UK. It is originally a result of crossing Tortoiseshell Persians with non-pedigree tortoiseshell shorthairs in the early 1950s. Then by introducing elements of the bicolor longhair, the wonderful white color was successfully arrived at.

Today this cat is one of the most popular of the Persian breeds but still rare as it breeds only female kittens.

To keep the breed true, male bicolor studs have to be used. However this also produces some interesting variations which are themselves becoming popular, such as the Dilute Calico which is known as the Blue tortoiseshell-and-white in the UK.

Because some genetic material has been acquired from the early matings with shorthairs the coat of the Calico is just as long and silky but not so prone to matting as other Persians.

Type:
cobby with short, thick legs; round head with short nose; large eyes

Facial characteristics:
head broad and round with pink nose pad; copper eye color

Coat:
basic black with red and cream patches, with vivid white front half but not the face

Color:
tortoiseshell-and-white

Temperament:
gentle, affectionate

Associated breeds:
other Persians

Colorpoint

Countries of origin: northern Asia, Turkey, Persia (now Iran)

Type:
cobby with short, thick legs; round head with short nose; large eyes

Facial characteristics:
round face showing both nose short and eyes large and round, bright sapphire blue eye color

Coat:
warm cream with markings to the points depending on color variety

Color:
seal, blue, chestnut brown, lavender, tabby, red

Temperament:
Persian gentleness combined with Siamese enthusiasm and spirit

Associated breeds:
other Persians; Siamese (for colorpoints)

The colorpoint is a popular breed successfully developed by combining the colorpoints of the Siamese with the body characteristics of the Persian. The breed is a recent development and was only standardized during the 1940s.

There are many varieties of colorpoints as there are in the Siamese cat world, with colors ranging from seal to tabby; chestnut brown to lavender; and red to blue. The facial characteristics should be the same as for any Persian— round and broad and no hint of the longer Siamese face. The eyes should be round and large and bright sapphire blue. The true colorpoint should have markings to the facial mask, ears, legs, feet, and tail. These are known as the points. The breed successfully combines not only coloring, but also the temperaments of the two breeds, with the gentleness of the Persian combined with a touch of the Siamese spirit.

above: **Colorpoint Persian.**

right: **Red Colorpoint Persian.**

Semi-longhaired breeds
Angora

Country of origin: Turkey

Type:
Persian

Facial characteristics:
medium wedge-shaped head;
long tapering nose; almond-
shaped eyes; large pointed ears,
wide at the base

Coat:
silky, medium length

Color:
pretty well any (see right)

Temperament:
gentle, fun-loving, friendly

Associated breeds:
none

Although at first sight it holds a lot of Persian similarities this is not a Persian. The Angora is a unique breed in that it has no close relative—it is a one-off. It is sometimes known as a semi-longhair as its coat is much shorter than a true Persian.

The Angora is a very ancient breed indeed. It originated in Turkey and was one of the first longhaired breeds to reach Europe in about the sixteenth century. Originally they were described as "dun-colored" or "ash-colored." In England they were known as French cats

and when the first Persians arrived these two breeds were intermingled a great deal—with some very odd results.

Gradually the popularity of the Angora waned as the Persian took hold, until, by the late 1940s, the breed had almost died out altogether. Luckily the state zoo of Turkey in Ankara had a breeding pair which they were happy to

above: **Lilac Turkish Angora.**

above: **Black Turkish Angora.**

lend to an American couple and, during the 1960s, an intensive and highly successful breeding program was undertaken with the result that the Angora was saved. It is now an extremely popular breed.

The first of the "new" Angoras to be bred were pure white but today many colors are accepted. In the UK a separate breeding program was undertaken to save the Angora which, in its own way, was just as successful. It used descendants of the original Angoras crossbred with Siamese to produce a British version of the Angora. This is almost identical to the American version except it has a much stronger meow due to its Siamese inheritance.

Looking after an Angora takes a lot less time and effort than caring for a Persian because their coat is much shorter and therefore easier to maintain. It has a naturally silky quality with a tendency to wave. The cat should have a thick ruff, and the long and tapering tail is carried curled. Colors now successfully and popularly being bred

include: white, black, blue (a blue-gray), black smoke (white with black tips to the guard hairs), blue smoke (white with blue tips), silver tabby (silver with black markings), red tabby (red with deeper red markings), brown tabby (brown with black tabby markings), blue tabby (blue-gray with darker blue tabby markings), calico (black, red, and white patches), and the bicolor Angora which has blue, black, red, white, and cream markings. The head is wedge-shaped, small to medium, with a long tapering nose. The hind legs are longer than the front legs. The eyes are almond shaped and orange (except in the white Angora when they are permitted to be blue or even odd-colored and the tabby Angora which can have green-hazel eyes). The overall body shape is slim and athletic. This is a lithe fun-loving cat that likes to play a lot. It is also very intelligent, with a gentle friendly disposition although it can show great aloofness toward strangers—until it gets to know them.

Balinese

Countries of origin: Thailand, USA

Type:
oriental, longhaired

Facial characteristics:
medium-size head with long tapering nose; large pointed ears, almond eyes, slanted toward the nose; very long tapering tail

Coat:
long, silky, no ruff

Color:
same as for Siamese

Temperament:
vocal, friendly, people-focused

Associated breeds:
Siamese

When Siamese were being bred successfully in the early part of the twentieth century, occasionally in litters there would appear a longhaired variety. These were often given away as pets and not bred from as they were considered "spoiled." They were obviously a genetic throwback to longhaired cats being used to help the Siamese breeding program. In the 1940s however a New York breeder spotted the potential and began a successful breeding program with a Californian breeder. The result is the longhaired Siamese—the Balinese.

The name Balinese comes, obviously, from the island of Bali but there is no evidence to suggest that the cat actually comes from there. The name is supposed to describe its lithe and graceful walk which is likened to the movements of a Balinese dancer. The cats were actually produced in the USA and were originally known as "Longhaired Siamese."

This is, to all extents and purposes, a Siamese with a longer coat. However the breed is slightly less vocal, a little more independent (although still heavily people-focused), and attains all the same true pure colorpoints as the Siamese itself. In the USA some colorpoint Balinese are known as Javanese such as the chestnut brown, the blue, and lavender frost points. There are few differences between versions found in the USA and the UK apart from the frost which is known as the lilac in the UK, and what is known as a Tortie point in the UK is called the Torbie in the USA. Also in the UK some varieties are known by different names than in the USA, such as their Lilac Tabby-point Balinese which is the Frost Lynx-point in the United States.

Caring for the Balinese is a relatively simple procedure, requiring nothing more than a light daily grooming and brushing the tail to enhance the plumed effect. As the coat is a longer version of the traditional Siamese coat there is no woolly undercoat which means fewer tangles and less matting.

The eye color is always blue and the colorpoints (the mask, ears, legs and feet, and tail) should be correct as for a Siamese. This is a very affectionate friendly cat with a happy disposition, and it is very active. Like the Siamese it can be very demanding and is very much a people-focused cat.

When being entered for shows there is some dispute as to whether they should be included under the category of longhairs or included in the oriental section. In the USA they are more likely to be classified as oriental cats, whereas in the UK they tend toward being a longhair.

above: **Seal Tabby Point Balinese.**

Birman

Country of origin: Burma

Type:
longhair

Facial characteristics:
round, broad face with round eyes
and medium-size ears

Coat:
creamy beige-gold with points of
the appropriate colorpoint;
white paws

Color:
US—seal, chestnut brown,
lavender, blue, red, cream, seal
tortie, blue tortie, tabby point, and
tabby tortie point; UK—seal,
chocolate, lilac, blue

Temperament:
gentle, affectionate, intelligent,
serene

Associated breeds:
none

bottom right: **Blue Point Birman.**

below: **Seal Point Birman.**

Whatever its history the Birman certainly seems capable of inspiring stories and legends wherever it goes. In Burma, where it originated, the legend goes that it got its four white paws by landing on the body of a dead holy man to protect it. He had been killed while defending a Buddhist temple against marauding invaders. The other priests were so inspired by the actions of the holy man's favorite pet that they successfully saw off the attackers and regained the temple. Since then the Birman has been venerated as a sacred animal, and the white paws are regarded as a sign of the cat's goodness.

In the West the legend is that the cat was presented to British officers as a thank you for defending a Buddhist temple during World War I. The first cat given as a gift was a heavily pregnant female who littered *en route* to France, so the breed became established there first. How much of this is true we'll probably never know. What we do know is that this inquisitive and affectionate cat was well established in the United States and the UK by the late 1960s.

If a Siamese was crossed successfully with a Persian, the Birman would probably look very much like the result. However this cat, while sharing many of the qualities of these breeds, isn't a cross. It's a truly independent breed with personality, characteristics, and physical attributes all of its own. It has silky fur which grooms easily and doesn't tangle. The white paws are comparatively easy to keep clean although they may need the

application of white grooming powder from time to time if you want to keep them really shining white—perhaps best left for when showing rather than for a pet. The Birman has a heavy ruff around its neck; its fur is long on its flanks, and it has a very bushy tail. The head is broad and strong without the pointedness of the Siamese or the pug-like appearance of the Persian. The eyes are almost round in shape and should always be a strong sapphire blue. There shouldn't be too much trace of oriental looks as this is almost a European cat in appearance with Siamese colorpoints.

In the US there are many colors, including red, cream, seal tortie, blue tortie, tabby point, and tabby tortie point. In the UK only four colors are officially recognized—seal-point, chocolate-point, lilac-point, and blue-point.

Its temperament is quiet but affectionate. The Birman has a rare quality about it, as if it knows something of its illustrious legendary past and of its somewhat holy nature. But then again it can be as silly as any kitten and not take itself too seriously. It is a very gentle loving cat which makes an excellent pet as well as a fine show animal.

Maine Coon

Country of origin: USA

Type:
longhaired

Facial characteristics:
large round head with tufted ears
and large round eyes

Coat:
long, full, and very thick,
longer on the tail

Color:
all colors permitted except
Siamese colorpoints

Temperament:
sociable, friendly, affectionate,
inventive, playful

Associated breeds:
Angoras

It is often thought that that the Maine Coon is a relatively recent "manmade" breed. That couldn't be more wrong. The Maine Coon is a very old breed indeed, although just exactly where its ancestry lies is a little lost in the mists of time. We do know that a tabby Maine Coon won the Best in Show in 1895 at the Madison Square Garden Cat Show but after that they went into a bit of a decline owing to the enormous popularity of the Persians and other longhaired breeds. It wasn't until 1953 that the Central Maine Coon Cat Club was formed to promote the breed.

right: **Red shaded Maine Coon.**

above: **Silver Tortie Tabby and White Maine Coon.**

So what are its origins? Nobody is absolutely sure. The two myths are that it is called a Maine Coon because it comes from the state of Maine, and was the result of crossbreeding between feral domestic cats and native racoons. Now we know that to be an impossibility as species cannot interbreed. Other stories tell of Marie Antoinette, wife of Louis XVI of France, sending her pet cats to be looked after in Maine when she was planning her own escape from the horrors of the guillotine during the French Revolution. Just why she would have pet Maine Coon cats no one ever quite explains and this story certainly seems to be a complete myth. The truth is that the delightful Maine Coon is probably the result of breeding between local domestic cats and Angoras brought ashore by visiting sailors aboard trading ships along the seaboard of Maine.

Once the breed went into a decline in the first half of the twentieth century, the cat was left to Maine folk to keep as pets. This probably did the breed a lot of good as it was left to its own devices, and it is stronger and more robust due to less administration from cat breeders.

This is a very large, playful, and friendly cat who is inventive, charming, and sociable. They are the heaviest of all domestic cats and can weigh as much as 30 lbs. They do love an outdoor life but will happily live indoors just so long as they are given plenty of exercise. They are very friendly to everyone, although they invariably select one member of the household to bond with completely—and they will make the object of their affection know pretty well who has been chosen as their special friend.

Maine Coons can be found in over 25 different colors—not all of which are permitted at shows—and they also have eight quite distinct tabby variations. They have a large well-muscled body with a broad chest and quite long legs. Their paws are heavily tufted and they have an enormous plumed tail which could be described as their breed feature.

Eye color varies depending on coat color but ranges from green to gold and copper. The only requirement of the eye color is that it should be very bright and that the eyes should be round with no hint of slantedness at all. Only the white Maine Coons have blue eyes.

Norwegian Forest Cat

Country of origin: Norway

Type:
longhaired

Facial characteristics:
triangular in shape with a
straight, long, and
wide nose

Coat:
dense and heavy, weatherproof,
oily guard hairs

Color:
any permitted except Siamese or
Burmese traits

Temperament:
friendly but independent

Associated breeds:
Persians and other longhairs

When the first Vikings went marauding and pillaging they brought home much gold and treasures—and the odd foreign cat from strange lands. These included longhairs from Asia and shorthairs from Europe. These imported cats naturally interbred with the domestic forest cats. The result is the truly magnificent Norwegian Forest Cat. This could be described as Norway's national cat and it embodies the spirit of those first Vikings.

It is a bold and intrepid cat with an extremely resourceful nature. It has been known to open latches on doors, climb precipitous cliffs, and it has the longest and sharpest claws on any domestic cat—and it can use them. It does, however, use them rarely as it is a friendly and well-loved pet. It loves being outdoors and can easily survive the harshest winter weather. It can adapt to life indoors but isn't really happy to do so unless it can get vast amounts of exercise. It takes to being a pet quite well but dislikes too much fussing or being groomed or pampered. This is a cat who knows its ancestry and isn't afraid of being a tough outdoor cat.

above: **Red Silver Tabby and White Norwegian Forest Cat.**

above: **Black and White Norwegian Forest Cat.**

As a show cat the Norwegian Forest Cat is a relative newcomer as breeders only got involved in the 1930s. They took domestic farm cats and began to develop the pedigree. Their basic stock was extremely hardy and the result is almost what they started with, with few improvements.

The coat is dense, thick, and weather-resistant. The woolly undercoat keeps the cat warm while the glossy topcoat can keep out rain and snow. It is described as a double coat. For a domestic pet it should require no grooming at all and only show cats need to be brushed to keep them in top form. This is a coat that needs very little attention.

The Norwegian Forest Cat has very strong legs and the hind ones should be longer than the front ones. It is a nimble and agile climber because of this feature and has an unusual characteristic when climbing—or rather when descending: it comes down head first and spirals down round a tree a little like a squirrel does.

The eyes should be large, almond shaped, and set wide apart. Eye colors can be any as long as they are suitable for the coat color. The brightness of the eye is more important than color among breeders. The body should be heavy, robust, and large, but not quite as large as a Maine Coon. Nevertheless this is still a big cat for a domestic pet.

The head should be triangular in shape with a straight, long, and wide nose. The nose and paw pads should correspond to the coat color. Colors vary as much as any other breed although any hint of Siamese colorpoints is disapproved of as are any Burmese traits.

Ragdoll

Country of origin: USA

This is a breed whose ancestry is very well documented. We even know the first mother of Ragdolls—Josephine. The breeder, Ann Baker from California, had Josephine from a kitten. She was a white longhaired cat of unknown breed, but may well have been a Persian, and she was unfortunately involved in a serious car accident. This left her with serious, permanent injuries. Nevertheless she became pregnant and the kittens were found to have strange characteristics—they were unusually placid and would go completely limp when picked up, like a ragdoll, hence the name.

They are also supposed to feel no pain, not to fight with any other cats, and to be immune from any fear. Whether these last attributes are true—or even wanted—remains unclear. What we do know is that the Ragdoll certainly can go limp and is very placid in nature.

The breed has caused some controversy but is now officially recognized throughout the world. Officially the breed was born by mating a white Persian queen with a seal-point Birman stud and then mating the kittens with sable Burmese. The Ragdoll now breeds true like-to-like and the resulting cat is large-bodied and heavy, with long legs and a broad chest. It has a large plumed tail, tufted paws, and the coat is heavy and long.

This business of the Ragdoll feeling no pain is quite interesting. Would we want a cat that could actually be free of

Type:
longhaired

Facial characteristics:
wedge-shaped with broad features

Coat:
long, or semi-long, dense, and heavy

Color:
lavender, chestnut brown, blue, and seal

Temperament:
affectionate, docile, placid

Associated breeds:
Persians, Burmese, Birman

below: **Seal Bi-color Ragdoll.**

all pain? Or would it be detrimental to the cat's very existence? After all if you can't feel pain you can't appreciate danger. However, most owners report that their own Ragdoll doesn't seem to be unable to feel pain and that they seem as normal as any other cat.

Ragdolls have a well-deserved reputation for being extremely tolerant and forgiving cats. They love to be groomed and petted, and make excellent indoor cats especially if the owner is at home all the time. The Ragdoll is not a cat to be left to its own devices and it really does need a lot of attention. Daily grooming is essential although the fur is relatively tangle free and doesn't mat; the cat itself seems to need regular attention and will go into a decline if it doesn't get it.

There are three distinct types of Ragdoll, depending on coat patterns, now being bred: the Bicolor which has a pale body with a white underbelly, a white chest and legs, and a dark mask, tail, and ears; the Colorpoint which has a pale body with darker points; and the Mitted. This has a white chest, chin, and bib, and all its paws are "mitted"; that is, they have the colorpoint extending from the elbows to the paws but the paws themselves are white. Otherwise it has the same coloring as the colorpoint. Permitted colors are the same as for Siamese with seal, blue, chestnut brown, and lavender dominating as favorites. The body color should be a pale ivory or light cream and the eye color is blue. The tail should be plumed and the coat thick and heavy.

below: **Blue Mitted Ragdoll.**
bottom left: **Lilac Point Ragdoll.**

Somali

Country of origin: USA

Type:
longhaired Abyssinian

Facial characteristics:
wedge-shaped, broad

Coat:
ticked, longhaired

Color:
ruddy, sorrel, lavender,
blue, silver

Temperament:
friendly, very affectionate

Associated breeds:
Abyssinian

below: **Usual Somali.**

The Somali is a longhaired Abyssinian—with a few interesting additions all of its own. For example the Abyssinian has three bands of color that form the ticking while the Somali has over 10 which give the hairs a very rich dense color. And whereas the Abyssinian can be a bit boisterous, the Somali is a very gentle and affectionate cat.

So how did it come about? The longhaired gene was carried by the Abyssinian for quite some time, possibly by out-crossing them to longhairs early on in the days of the breed. When longhaired Abyssinians appeared occasionally in litters they were regarded as "spoiled" and given away as pets, but once they had become fully grown and truly quite magnificent their breed possibilities were recognized.

The longhaired gene was probably introduced during the 1930s and the breeders got to work in the 1960s to get the breed to produce like-to-like, which they managed successfully and the breed was given recognition in the 1970s. Today the breed is found throughout the world but, for some strange reason, it seems to have really taken off in Australia where it has completely eclipsed the true Abyssinian.

This is a ticked longhaired cat of quite some beauty. It has a rich non-matting coat which requires little attention apart from an occasional grooming. The tail has a full brush and is

There are two most commonly bred varieties: the Ruddy (known in the UK as the Usual), which has a golden coat ticked with darker brown or black; and the Red (known in the UK as the Sorrel), which has a warm copper-colored coat ticked with chestnut brown. A relatively new breed is the Silver Sorrel which doesn't have the chestnut brown ticking but is uniformly sorrel all over with a pale undercoat. Breeders are also producing lavenders and blues.

This is a fun-loving affectionate cat which prefers an indoor life and a lot of attention. They make excellent pets because they are extremely friendly although prone to becoming overweight because they do like to eat—a lot. They are not able to withstand the cold very well despite their long coat and they prefer a pampered sheltered existence.

carried proud and erect; it should be thick at the base, slightly tapering, and very long.

The head is wedge shaped but not too oriental and the nose is medium sized. The eyes are large, almond shaped, and can be hazel, amber, or green. Overall the cat should be strong looking with none of the Siamese delicateness nor the Persian heaviness.

above: **Blue/Silver Somali.**
below: **Sorrel Somali.**

Tiffanie

Countries of origin: UK, USA

above: **Brown Smoke Tiffanie.**

Type:
longhaired Burmese

Facial characteristics:
rounded; wide-set ears

Coat:
smooth, ruff around
neck, plumed tail

Color:
sable (USA), any same
as Burmese (UK)

Temperament:
friendly though cautious with
strangers, playful

Associated breeds:
Burmese, Himalayans

The delightful Tiffanie is a bit of a by-product and was regarded as undesirable when first produced. Breeders in the UK were trying to produce a solid chocolate (chestnut brown) Himalayan (now called the Kashmir) when they got a longhaired Burmese. This was a result of mating Himalayans with Burmese; the litters contained some of the longhaired variety and a few solid chocolates, which is what was wanted. American breeders spotted the potential and developed the breed more fully.

The cat is sometimes called Tiffany in the UK, but it's the same cat as the Tiffanie nevertheless. In the USA it is only allowed in its pure sable coloring while in the UK it is allowed in any color permutation that is also found in the Burmese.

The coat is medium to long and quite smooth. The face is fox-like with round eyes. The body is the typical Burmese shape—rounded and sturdy—although UK Tiffanies do tend toward a slightly more oriental look being somewhat sleeker and more lithe. The head is rounded, with a broad short muzzle, and the nose is small and short. The eyes are medium in size, set well apart, and slightly rounded at the outside edges. The coat should be long and "ragged" in appearance, although it should be silky to the touch.

It is a very gentle affectionate cat with a curious bird-like call. It is very vocal and will call to its owner to get attention. It has quite an outgoing personality and is very inquisitive. It likes to play and explore, but it's very much an indoor cat and doesn't like the cold.

The Tiffanie seems to have adopted all the best characteristics of its very mixed ancestry. For instance although it calls and is very vocal, its voice isn't as strident as a Siamese—nor quite so demanding. It has inherited its sturdy body from the Burmese, its beautiful fur coloring from the Himalayan, and its playfulness from the Siamese.

Unfortunately the longhair gene it has also inherited is recessive, and fewer and fewer kittens are born into each litter. Thus it is, and is likely to remain, a relatively rare breed which is maintained and kept in existence by the efforts of some very dedicated breeders.

In the UK some wonderful color ranges are found including the Brown Smoke which has a creamy/chocolate body, with much darker points and an almost marbled effect. There are also the lilac and the red which have an overall coat color of either lilac or red, and are as beautiful as the American sable. In all cases the eye color should be golden with no hint of oriental eye shape; instead the eyes should be large and round.

Turkish Van

Countries of origin: Turkey, UK, USA

Type:
longhaired

Facial characteristics:
short blunt head, triangular
in shape

Coat:
silky, long, with
no undercoat

Color:
red-and-white, cream-and-white,
black-and-white

Temperament:
friendly, affectionate, playful

Associated breeds:
other European cats

right: **Auburn and white
Turkish Van.**
below: **Cream and White
Turkish Van.**

The Turkish Van takes its name from the region in Turkey where it was first noticed—and then taken to the UK to be bred from—the magnificent Lake Van. In the UK it is known simply as the Turkish cat, while in the USA it is the Turkish Van and also the Turkish Swimming cat which may tell you something about what it likes to do in its spare time—swimming.

In 1955 an English cat breeder, Laura Lushington, was on holiday with a friend in the Lake Van region of Turkey when she spotted the native Turkish cat swimming in the lake. Quite unable to believe what she had seen she managed to acquire a breeding pair and returned to the UK with them. A breeding program was introduced and she had to import other cats from Turkey to complete it which she did successfully, and in 1969 the breed was given official recognition. The Turkish Van was also introduced quite separately into the USA a little later and the two breeds are independent but, to all extents and purposes, identical.

The first Turkish Vans were nervous and highly strung but that trait has been successfully deleted, and the modern Turkish Van is hugely playful and very affectionate, bold, and socially well adjusted. The Turkish Van, as well as being a swimming cat, also has one other curious characteristic—in the summer it loses so much fur it becomes a shorthair for a few months. This is because the region in Turkey where it originated is subject to very hot summers and cold winters, thus creating a cat which has warm long fur in the winter to combat the cold and a shorthaired coat in the summer to help it stay cool. This may also be why it has taken to swimming—to cool down in the cold water of Lake Van.

It is a medium to heavy build of cat with no trace of oriental in it. It is a European cat in that it has a sturdy body and a long feathery tail. It also has two curious markings on its forehead—these are thumb-size spots of color which are said, by the Turks, to be the thumbprints of Allah himself who bent down to bless the cat for its beauty. Allah held the cat's head in his hands as he kissed it, leaving the sacred impressions.

The coat colors usually seen are red (auburn in the UK), cream, and black-and-white although recently tortoiseshell-and-white cats have been bred. The body color should be creamy white with the two small marks on the head in red, cream, or black, and the tail the same. Eye color is usually a pale amber although odd-colored cats do appear in litters from time to time with the usual deafness in the blue eye-color side.

This is an affectionate cat which will swim quite readily, given the opportunity to do so. It likes to be groomed although it doesn't need to be as much as some breeds. The silky topcoat has no undercoat, which makes it very easy to look after because it doesn't mat or tangle.

Shorthaired breeds

For a number of reasons the shorthaired cat is much more likely to survive in the wild than a longhaired breed. Longhaired cats can become tangled and matted more easily than shorthaired cats, and that long fur makes better homes for parasites. Their wounds don't heal as fast nor as well, and they are more prone to skin diseases than shorthairs. They lose fights more often as their adversaries

above: **American Shorthair Brown Classic Tabby.**

have a better chance of gripping them and thus defeating them. That is probably why the longhair gene is recessive while the shorthair gene is dominant. It's Nature's way of making sure the best survives. Obviously with modern breeding techniques we can have both longhairs and shorthairs in abundance, but it also shows why shorthaired cats are more common and tend to live longer, making them, perhaps, more suitable as pets.

Shorthaired cats are divided into three classifications for the purposes of breeding and showing—American shorthairs, British shorthairs, and Oriental or Foreign shorthairs. The American shorthairs include the American Wirehair while the British shorthairs include the British Spotted Shorthair, and the British Tabby Shorthair.

The Oriental shorthairs include such breeds as the Siamese, the Korat, and the Havana. We will look at all these in more detail in a moment but you might need to know why there are such classifications and what they are based on.

The American shorthaired cat developed from the British but has become leaner and larger than its British cousins which tend to be fatter, rounder, and smaller. The Orientals are, in general, more lithe, and more "oriental"-looking in that they have slanted eyes and wedge-shaped heads. The European shorthaired cats, such as the Chartreux, which comes from France and has been a popular breed there since the sixteenth century, come under the same classification as for British shorthaired cats and are identical in their characteristics.

The term "oriental," when applied to shorthaired cats, doesn't necessarily mean they originated in the Far East, although quite a few did. Instead it is a term used to describe the particular type of cat which is lithe, and slim, and has large ears, slanted eyes, and a pointed face. Oriental shorthaired cats, such as the Siamese, are bred on both sides of the Atlantic—in fact worldwide—and are extremely popular because they combine exotic appeal with the classic show cat look, and make very good and playful pets.

For many British cat owners, the idea that their pet "moggie" may indeed have a long and glorious pedigree may seem unusual. British shorthairs are very common and popular, and are usually acquired as pets from friends or local shops. Also the British cat breeding population took a bit of a downturn during World War II, owing to the difficulties of keeping breeds going during the hostilities. Now, however, the British breeding fraternity is fully recovered, extremely widespread, and very intense. Cat shows are a popular part of British life and the notion of pedigrees for British shorthaired cats is gaining some recognition.

American shorthaired cats have always enjoyed a widespread devotion because they are not indigenous to the USA. They had to be smuggled in—or arrived because they were conveyed by accident—and bred carefully. We will take a look at the American shorthaired cats first.

American Shorthairs

Countries of origin: USA, UK

We know for certain that Christopher Columbus took cats with him to the Americas, as did the stalwart souls aboard the *Mayflower*. What we don't know is what happened to them. We know that by the beginning of the twentieth century there were enough "native" shorthaired cats for an English breeder to send over a pedigree British Red Tabby Shorthair to start a breeding program.

This cat, Belle, was the first cat to be registered with the Cat Fanciers' Association. Other British pedigrees were sent over and the name Shorthair was chosen for the new breed. They were known as Domestic Shorthair for a long time, but by 1966 a final name of American Shorthair had been arrived at, and a set of standards was drawn up to determine the breed characteristics. They are still called Domestic Shorthair in Canada.

What determines an American Shorthair and why is it different than its British cousins? The USA version of the shorthair is a muscular cat with well-developed shoulders and chest. It is strong in the leg and with a more rectangular head than the British version which is round. The eyes are set well apart and are round. It has large ears, a short coat without any white spots or "oriental" markings.

Type:
shorthair

Facial characteristics:
rectangular head with large round eyes and large ears

Coat:
dense, thick, short, hard

Color:
any apart from oriental colorpoints, chestnut brown, and lavender

Temperament:
friendly, calm, robust, affectionate

Associated breeds:

BROWN TABBY

this has a base coat color of bright copper/brown with dense black markings; the backs of the legs should be black; paw pads should be black or brown; nose pad should be brick red; eyes bright golden

RED TABBY

this has a base coat color of red with rich deep red markings to make up the tabby; paw pads and nose pad should all be brick red, and eyes a bright golden

CAMEO TABBY

this has a base coat color of creamy white with red markings; nose and paw pads should be rose, and the eyes golden

CREAM TABBY

this has a base coat color of a very pale cream with darker cream markings; paw and nose pads should be pink, and the eyes bright gold

SILVER TABBY

this is one of the most striking of all the American shorthairs, and could be said to sum up all that is best of the breed. It has a base coat color of silver with deep black markings; paw pads should be black; nose leather should be pink, and the eyes green or hazel

below: **Blue Tabby American Shorthair.**

VARIETY	COAT COLOR
White	Pure white
Black	Jet black
Blue	Pale blue/gray
Red	Deep rich red
Calico	White with black and red patches
Van	White with Turkish Van cat markings
Smoke	Undercoat depending on color, such as pale blue for Blue Smoke, and black markings

right: **Silver Tabby American Shorthair and** bottom: **Red Tabby American Shorthair.**

They are a tough breed, evolving from working farm cats and having had to survive some pretty harsh weather conditions. They are friendly and affectionate. They make good show cats and are also excellent as pets because they are very good with children and very tolerant. They can be almost any color you can think of—except oriental, that is, having points—and chestnut brown and lavender versions are frowned upon by breeders although they do crop up as domestic pets from time to time.

Colors range from white to black, silver to tabby, cameo to patched, smoke to calico, and bicolor to "van." They take color well and retain it well.

Of all the American Shorthairs, the tabbies seem to be the most popular, and they come in a very wide range of colors.

As with British Shorthairs the tabbies are divided into "classic" and "mackerel," with the classic markings being rings in dark bands and the mackerel having thin pencil lines of dark markings instead.

Eye color for all American Shorthairs should be golden except for the Silver tabby and the Shaded Silver which are allowed a blue-green eye color, and the Chinchilla Silver which is allowed to have emerald-green eyes. All the other colors are listed here with a brief description of their coat color.

All in all the American Shorthair is a resilient, happy breed of cat who adapts easily to life as it finds it. It is affectionate, good with children, long lived, and robust.

British Shorthairs

British Black Shorthair

Country of origin: UK

Is this the cat of your nightmares or your dreams? It all depends on where you live. In some places the black cat is lucky but in others it is unlucky. But the black cat—especially the British Black Shorthair—has had more bad press than any other. This is the witch's familiar, the pagan symbol of the Horned God, the agent of the devil, and harbinger of disease, ill omen, and disaster.

In the Middle Ages so many black cats were cruelly killed that it's a wonder any survived. Perhaps that's why so many people consider this cat lucky—lucky enough to have come through and be so beautiful and popular today.

The first British Black Shorthair pedigrees were shown in London at the Crystal Palace cat shows in the late nineteenth century. They were bred by using the very best domestic pets that could be found. The result is a very handsome cat with a good-natured approach to life and extreme intelligence.

The pedigree version of the British Black Shorthair has two main differences from its domestic cousin. First the body shape must conform to the set standard of stocky and muscular rather than lithe and slim—which is what most pet black cats are. It must also have beautiful bright orange eyes rather than the more common green eyes of the pet cat. Obviously this standard is hard to achieve but it doesn't discount the domestic pet in any way—merely lays down a standard for show cats and pedigrees.

The paws should be large, round, and with black paw pads. The legs should be short and well proportioned. The tail is short and thick. The overall body color should be uniform with no hint of tabby; it should be jet or coal black with no white hairs anywhere. The face should be round and broad, with a short straight nose, large round eyes of bright orange, and a well-developed chin. The ears are medium size with round tips.

The coat color will fade to a rust color if the cat lies out in the sun too much. On the other hand, some kittens are born with a rust-colored coat which usually develops into a full black one within six months. To get the coat looking very sleek and glossy, you can rub the cat with a soft leather cloth but, apart from that, it needs little in the way of grooming.

Occasionally tortoiseshell cats will produce black kittens and the British Black Shorthair is used in the breeding program of tortoiseshell cats to strengthen the line.

This is a friendly cat although it may be prone to being a little independent. It is good with children and very gentle. It is a highly intelligent cat which, at times, seems to have an almost telepathic bond with its owner.

Type:
British shorthair

Facial characteristics:
round, broad; medium-size ears;
round orange eyes

Coat:
short and dense

Color:
only black permitted
no varieties

Temperament:
gentle, intelligent, affectionate

Associated breeds:
other British shorthairs

British Blue Shorthair

Country of origin: UK

Type:
shorthair

Facial characteristics:
round and broad; medium-size
ears with rounded tips; bright
orange eyes

Coat:
short, thick, dense, no white or
tabby markings

Color:
blue

Temperament:
friendly, gentle, a little
lazy, charming

Associated breeds:
Chartreux, other
British shorthairs

Although the British Blue Shorthair is a very long-established breed, it has only recently reached the peak of its development. The first blues were shown at the London Crystal Place cat shows at the end of the nineteenth century, when they caused quite a stir and were very popular. They were bred using the best domestic pet blues that could be found and were very true to their type and standards.

During World War II the breed fell into disarray owing to the problems with the hostilities, and after the war attempts were made to bring the breed up to standard by introducing blue longhairs into the stock. This was a disaster because the coat became far too long to qualify as a genuine shorthair. It took a long time to get it right and only during the 1950s was the breed considered worth showing again. Since then it has become the most popular shorthaired cat—probably in the world, not just in the UK.

Over the decades the coat color standard has changed. Originally it was a dark slate-blue but that has now changed to a lighter blue. There should be no tabby markings in the coat and no white hairs are permitted. The body shape should conform to the British standard—strong and muscular, a stockily built cat with no trace of slim oriental looks. The tail should be short and thick, and the legs also short but well proportioned. The paw pads should be blue, as should the nose leather. The eyes should be bright orange, round, and set wide apart. The ears should be medium size and have rounded tips. This is a cat with almost the perfect temperament to be a pet. It is playful—some say to the point of naughtiness—gentle, affectionate, and independent but people-focused. It is robust, stable and well balanced. It is good with children, long-lived, and happy to curl up in front of the fire. What more could you ask of a cat?

In the United States a somewhat sturdier cat standard is set, with more gray in its coat and a slightly longer, more oriental face is allowed. Apart from that though, the cat is the same animal.

In France it is known as the Chartreux. This cat was bred by the monks of the La Grande Chartreuse monastery, famous for its liqueur. There is some dispute as to whether the Chartreux and the British Blue Shorthair should be given independent categories but most breeders now agree it is the same cat, produced by different routes but arriving at a common destination—the blue shorthair.

To keep the blue standard high it is often necessary to outcross with blue longhairs and black shorthairs. This keeps the breed fresh and the gene pool revitalized.

British Cream Shorthair

Country of origin: UK

Type:
British shorthair

Facial characteristics:
broad and round; eyes orange or copper (US); medium ears with rounded tips; cream nose leather

Coat:
thick and dense

Color:
pale cream with no tabby or white

Temperament:
very good natured and extremely fond of owners

Associated breeds:
other British shorthairs

An all-over cream-colored cat is really hard to produce. Consequently the British Cream Shorthair is a two-tone cream cat. Within its fur there will be faint tabby markings, but these should be as pale and as minimal as possible. The overall color should also be as pale as possible. There should be no white hairs in the coat. The tabby gene is dominant so it comes as no surprise to learn that this cat is rare, difficult to produce, and equally difficult to maintain. Any adverse weather conditions—too hot, too cold—will cause the tabby markings to appear in the coat.

Using tortoiseshells to produce the red color (cream is only a version of red but very diluted) doesn't work particularly well because the tortoiseshell red tends to produce a cream that isn't quite right—it's been described as too "hot." The ideal color for a British Cream Shorthair should be the color of English Devonshire cream—which is very hard to achieve.

This is a relatively recent breed and was only recognized in the 1920s. Prior to that any cream shorthairs which appeared in litters of tortoiseshells were regarded as spoiled and given away. Besides which, no one knew how to duplicate the coat color and any produced were entirely accidental. Today we understand breeding and genetics much better and we can design virtually any color coat we desire. The British Cream Shorthair first became widely noticed— and popular— once the breeding program was well established in the 1950s and 1960s. Since then, despite the problems about getting the coat color right, it has remained a very desirable cat.

Coat length should be short and dense, as per the standard for any British shorthair, and the tail should be short and thick. The head should be round and broad. The ears should be medium size with rounded tips. The eyes should be round, large, and coppery gold, or bright orange in the UK. For a little while, green-eyed creams were allowed, but no longer—they have been relegated to the realms of domestic pets only. The paws should be large and round with pink paw pads—and the same color nose leather of course.

To produce a really fine example it is best to mate a female blue-cream with a male blue or a male cream, and then select only the palest kittens to include in a breeding program.

If the cream was produced from the red tabby it would seem logical that a self-colored red would be next on the list. Unfortunately this has never been achieved because the dominant tabby gene always comes through and the cat is quite simply merely a Red Tabby. But what a magnificent cat it would be if it could be produced!

British White Shorthair

Country of origin: UK

Type:
British shorthair

Facial characteristics:
broad and round with medium-size ears and large round eyes of the appropriate color—blue, orange, or both

Coat:
thick, dense, and pure white

Color:
white

Temperament:
friendly, affectionate, generally undemanding

Associated breeds:
other British shorthairs

The British White, like the Persian White, comes in three distinct varieties which are all based on eye color: the Orange Eyed which as its name suggests has orange eyes (UK) and copper eyes (US); the Blue Eyed which has blue eyes, and this one is prone to deafness as the blue eye gene is defective in this respect; and the Odd Eyed which has odd colored eyes—one orange and one blue. Any deafness in this cat will be on the blue-eyed side.

Like most British shorthairs this cat was bred by taking British domestic pets at the end of the nineteenth century and subjecting them to a thorough and intensive breeding program. The resulting pedigrees were shown in London and quickly became popular. The White Shorthair was no exception. Consequently it retains a lot of its early genetic material which means this cat is no pampered show item but a rough and tough cat that is more than capable of taking care of itself. You can tell a pedigree from a real domestic pet white

by the eye color—pets have green eyes which is not permitted in show cats of this variety.

Originally the white was only available as a show cat with blue eyes but because of the deafness problem an orange-eyed version was developed. The result was good, with no deafness in the orange-eyed version but the odd-eyed variety came into being which, although not as deaf as its blue-eyed cousin, is still prone to hearing loss. This is not a good thing because the cat relies heavily on its hearing for hunting, but perhaps this doesn't pertain to modern show cats.

To achieve a perfect white coat is not easy, as you would imagine. Often in the kittens you can see a genetic throwback, with stripes of blue or black on their forehead. These usually fade by about six months but they are quite interesting in that they tell you something of the kittens' long and colorful genetic past. The coat should be snowy white, very thick and dense, and with no hint of gray or cream in it. The body should conform to the British standard of short, stocky, and muscular.

The head should be broad and round with a well-developed chin, a straight nose, medium-size round tipped ears set well apart, and large round eyes of either blue, orange, or both. The tail should be thick and short and the legs short and well proportioned. The paws should be large with pink pads, and the nose leather should also be pink. The temperament of this cat can best be described as robust in all it does—sleeps well, eats heartily, plays vigorously, loves wholeheartedly, and gives of itself completely.

British Bicolor Shorthair

Country of origin: UK

If you are visiting England and you see a pretty cat wandering through a leafy garden, chances are it'll be a bicolor British shorthair. However, it probably won't be a pedigree. A non-pedigree bicolor is probably one of the commonest cats in the UK but a true pedigree version one of the rarest. It is so common as a "moggie"—a domestic pet—that its potential as a show cat was overlooked for a very long time. In fact it has only recently been recognized as a breed in its own right.

The standards set for the breed in 1966 are very stringent and the judges are harsh in their disapproval of any cats that fail to meet the mark. Ideally you have to have a cat in which the white takes up no more than half of the body color, or, even better exactly one third. The rest has to be unbroken color of a non-tabby sort, such as black (these are known as Magpies), red, cream, or blue.

The face must have a color mask covering the eyes, with a white bar extending up from the nose to a blaze on the forehead. The eyes must be round, large, and copper or orange in color with no hint of a green rim. The ears are medium in size and round tipped. The nose should be round and broad with either a pink color to the leather or a color which matches the coat color. The coat fur should be short and very dense, with no hint of tabby or any white hairs appearing in the other color. The tail should be the other color, that is, not white. All four legs should be white and the "self" color should start just behind the shoulders, extend backward to the base of the tail, and include the tail. The ideal bicolor has a white chest, throat and chin. That's about it—too much white debars the cat from professional showing.

The cream-and-white variety is the most appealing but all of them are charming as kittens, and they mature early. The bicolor is a very friendly easy-to-look-after sort of cat which likes being pampered but is still basically a tough cat with a liking for the outdoor life. They are good with children.

The modern British Bicolor Shorthair is a breed which is about to take off color-wise as breeders are now beginning to experiment with lots of other varieties, including shaded, spotted, and tipped versions.

Originally the bicolor had to have a mask like a Dutch rabbit—split exactly up the center of the face, and with the white blaze extending back beyond the face to the very back of the head. But as this proved too difficult to replicate, it was dropped. Likewise the disapproval of tabby markings, white hairs in the self color, and too much white are all breed standards which look likely to change in the not-too-distant future.

Type:
shorthair

Facial characteristics:
broad, rounded, short straight nose

Coat:
dense, thick, short

Color:
black-and-white, cream-and-white, red-and-white, blue-and-white

Temperament:
friendly, even-tempered, intelligent

Associated breeds:
other British shorthairs

below: **British Cream/White Bicolor.**

British Blue-cream Shorthair

Country of origin: UK

Type:
British shorthair

Facial characteristics:
round, broad, with a
short straight nose, rounded ears,
and bright copper/orange eyes

Coat:
thick, dense

Color:
blue-cream only. In the
USA the colors should be clearly
defined and distinct, whereas in
the UK the mingling should be
subtle and gradual

Temperament:
gentle, sleepy,
affectionate, friendly

Associated breeds:
other British shorthairs

The British Blue-cream Shorthair is a relatively new cat, introduced during the late 1950s. It was bred by crossing British Blue Shorthairs with British Cream Shorthairs. In the USA the two colors should be clearly defined, but in the UK the two colors should subtly blend into each other. Australia adopts the same standards as the British.

There should be no tabby markings in the coat and no white hairs anywhere on the body. The fur should be short and dense, and the cream hairs will be finer than the blue ones. This may necessitate more regular grooming than other British Shorthairs demand.

The paw pads should be blue or cream, or a mixture of the two. The nose leather should be blue. In the USA the eyes are a golden copper color, but in the UK they are bright orange.

The British standard seeks a stocky and muscular body but in the USA a slightly more lithe body shape is called for. The USA cat has a slightly more oriental look about it, especially around the face which is allowed to be longer than its round-faced British counterpart.

The paler the coat, the more desirable the cat will be as a show cat, and there seems to be a move toward a very pale cream with a slightly darker blue. The blue-cream is actually a dilute version of the tortoiseshell and was bred by crossing blues and creams, blues and tortoiseshells, and creams and tortoiseshells. In litters you will find solid colored kittens as well as blue-creams because, unfortunately, the color gene is sex linked and there are no adult blue-cream males. Thus you are always obliged to outcross with a stud of a single color to achieve the blue-cream, and you will have to expect solid-colored kittens as a result of this. However the kittens are always delightful and if you use a pedigree single color stud they are just as valid in their own color classification.

The popularity of the blue-cream is probably a result of its somewhat indolent personality. This really is the sleeping cat, the cushion cat, the lying-by-the-fire cat. It can be playful and adventurous, it's just that it prefers a somewhat more laid-back existence. It's always where you last left it—sleeping. When it is awake it is alert, curious, and hungry.

British Smoke Shorthair

Country of origin: UK

Type:
shorthair

Facial characteristics:
broad, round

Coat:
thick, dense

Color:
black, blue

Temperament:
gentle, affectionate

Associated breeds:
none

below: **Black British Smoke Shorthair.**

Who can fail to be impressed with a British Smoke's coat? That delightful flash of brilliant silver as it wakes and turns active. The undercoat is pure white with a topcoat of either blue or black, and it is this undercoat—seen through the topcoat—which gives this cat its unusual appearance.

It is a relatively new breed and was produced by crossing self-colored British shorthairs, such as the blue and the black, with British Shorthair Silver Tabbies. And, although this has been possible for nearly a century, it is only fairly recently that the breed has produced true.

There are only two varieties recognized by all cat associations—the black smoke and the blue smoke. However there are many other varieties. Some of these are recognized by some associations while others are not. For instance there is the British Shorthair Tortoiseshell Smoke which is now mostly accepted in the UK but still awaits official acceptance in the USA.

British Spotted Shorthair

Country of origin: UK

Type:
British shorthair

Facial characteristics:
broad, round, with medium-size ears with round tips, large round eyes, and a short straight nose

Coat:
thick and dense

Color:
brown, red, silver

Temperament:
gentle, affectionate, sweet natured

Associated breeds:
other British shorthairs

Technically the British Spotted Shorthair is a tabby. It is really a remarkably beautiful cat. It was first produced as early as 1880 and shown at London cat shows at Crystal Palace during the 1880s, where it was well received and became extremely popular. It looked exotic and wild, unusual and beautiful, and it held the public's affection until the time when true exotic orientals, in the shape of the Siamese, arrived on the scene. The British Spotted Shorthairs then remained out of favor until the 1960s when it returned in some force. Luckily dedicated breeders had kept the breed alive and well.

So what makes it a tabby? It is a mackerel tabby with the pencil markings broken up into spots. It completes the tabby trilogy of rings, lines, and spots.

The spots on a Spotted can be round, oval, rectangular, even rosette shaped—just as long as they are clearly defined. Also the coat should have no bars, stripes, or lines in it, except for the "M" on the forehead. The spots don't have to be of the same color as the base coat—but there are blue spots on a Spotted Blue, and red spots on a Spotted Red. However, you also find black spots on a Spotted Silver, and black spots on a Spotted Brown.

above: **British Red Spotted Shorthair.**

above: **British Silver Spotted Shorthair.**

The head should be large and round, with a well-developed chin. The nose should be short and straight. The nose leather should be brick-red or black. The legs should be short, but in proportion; the paws large and round, with brick-red or black pads (these should match the nose leather color). The tail should be short and thick with a tip of the same color as the spots. The back should have a broken stripe—the cat is penalized by judges if this stripe is unbroken. The tail should have broken rings, and, again, there is a penalty faulting if the rings are continuous around the tail.

Eye color is orange (copper US) except for the Silver Spotted which is required to have green (UK) or hazel (US) eyes, which should be rimmed with black.

The body should conform to the British standard of short, muscular, and generally stocky.

There are many varieties of the British Spotted but the ones which are most popular and accepted are the silver, the brown, and the red. This is a sweet-natured affectionate cat, although it has been accused of greed before now. Whether this is true or not can be discovered from individual owners.

British Tabby Shorthair

Country of origin: UK

Of all the cats in the world, it is the tabby which sums up the very epitome of "catness." It has been painted on the tombs of Egyptian kings and queens, written about by poets, featured in children's cartoons and plays, been the subject of photographs and postcards, and generally been loved by thousands of generations of cat owners. It is the very cat itself, developed from wildcats and domesticated cats thousands of years ago. It is the perfectly camouflaged cat with the dominant gene.

Where did the name come from? It came from Baghdad in Iraq. There is a native trading quarter in Baghdad called the *Attabiya* where you can buy a particularly beautiful striped cloth known in the West as *tabbi silk*, and it is from this cloth that our much-loved tabby cat gets its name.

There are three distinct types of tabby—the classic with rings, the mackerel with pencil stripes, and the spotted with spots. We have looked at the spotted so we will deal with the classic and the mackerel.

The Classic

The markings are rings or spirals of dark color on a lighter background. This is the traditional tabby marking and the cat should have a "butterfly" shape on its shoulders from which three stripes appear and run down the spine to the tail. The tail itself should be ringed with dark color and have a tip of dark color. The cat should have two spirals—one on each flank—known as "oysters," and also narrow rings around the chest. The belly should be spotted and there should be a

very distinct "M" on the forehead. The legs should also be ringed but the paws must be clear of dark markings.

The Mackerel

The markings are called "pencils," and are thinner and straighter than on a classic tabby with no rings or spirals. The forehead should carry the "M" and the lines should then run up over the top of the head and down the spine. The legs should be barred and the paws must be clear of dark markings. Along the spine the lines should run together to form a "saddle" of dark fur. The tail should be barred and the tip dark.

Eye color in both types should be orange (UK) and golden-copper (US). The ears are medium size with rounded tips. The body should conform to the British standard for shorthairs which is sturdy, stocky, and muscular. Colors recognized by breeders as show cats are brown, red, silver, cream, and blue, while the UK recognizes brown, red, and silver.

The temperament of the British tabby couldn't be better. It is gentle and affectionate, brave, daring, and independent—but still very loving. It likes to sleep and eat well, and is a friendly and charming pet to have around children.

Type:
British shorthair

Facial characteristics:
broad and round with medium size ears, rounded at the tips; large round eyes, orange colored (UK) and copper/golden (US)

Coat:
thick and dense

Color:
brown, red, silver (UK), and cream and blue in the US as well

Temperament:
friendly and charming, a delightful cat

Associated breeds:
other British shorthairs

above: **Brown Classic British Tabby Shorthair.**
below: **Red Mackerel British Tabby Shorthair.**

British Tipped Shorthair

Country of origin: UK

The British Tipped Shorthair is a very recent addition to the British shorthair cat stable as it was only introduced and recognised in the late 1970s. Originally it was called the Chinchilla Shorthair but the name was changed and it is only known now as the Tipped Shorthair. It was bred by crossing British Blue Shorthairs with British Smoke Shorthairs and the breeding program was complex and long. It is sometimes referred to as a shorthaired version of the longhaired Chinchilla or Cameo Persian, but it really is an original shorthair.

Ideally it should have a white undercoat and the fur on its flanks, back, head, ears, and tail should be tipped with color—any color of the recognized color cats such as black, blue, cream, red, chestnut brown, golden, tortie, and lavender.

It is a slightly more slender cat than the normal British shorthair, although it is still described as solid and cobby, but it is definitely lighter boned than normal. The head is broad and round, with small ears that are widely set apart and very neat looking. The coat should be short and very thick, with the tipped hairs giving a sparkling appearance. The eyes are large, round, and deep orange (UK) and copper (US) and rimmed with rose except in the black-tipped where they are allowed to be green and should be rimmed with black. The paw pads should be pink or match the tipping and the nose leather should do the same. There should be no tabby markings, although faint vestigial tail rings are allowed. The chin, chest, and stomach should all be white.

This is a very sweet-natured cat with an affectionate and generally undemanding personality. It is equally at home with children as with breeders, and makes a good pet as well as a beautiful show cat.

The most popular of the tipped shorthairs definitely seems to be the black tipped. Genetically this is actually a silver variety. The tips should be restricted to the very ends of the hairs and the undercoat should be so pale as to appear to be pure white. The eyes can only be green and they should be rimmed with black. The nose pad should be pink and the paw pads black or pink. This is a beautiful cat with a grace and elegance all of its own. It is followed closely by the cream tipped. This is a cream tipped on white cat with orange eyes (copper in the US). It also is a very beautiful cat and a fairly recent new breed.

below: **British Black Tipped Shorthair.**

Type:
British shorthair

Facial characteristics:
broad and round with a straight nose; small ears with round tips and set wide apart; large round eyes in orange (UK), copper (US), or green in the case of the black tipped

Coat:
thick and dense; white undercoat tipped with color

Color:
any allowed as for other British shorthairs with the inclusion of lavender and chestnut brown

Temperament:
sweet natured, friendly, affectionate

Associated breeds:
other British shorthairs

British Tortoiseshell Shorthair

Country of origin: UK

Type:
British shorthair

Facial characteristics:
round and broad with a straight nose and medium-size ears; large round eyes

Coat:
thick and dense

Color:
tortoiseshell, tortoiseshell-and-white; blue tortoiseshell-and-white

Temperament:
gentle, affectionate, greedy

Associated breeds:
other British shorthairs

below: **British Tortoiseshell Shorthair.**

In the UK this might be described as the typical English farm cat. Tortoiseshell cats make good mousers and excellent hunters in general so it's no surprise to find them gainfully employed on farms. That they hunt well may be to do with the fact that they are all female and need to provide for their frequent litters, as they also mature early and breed prolifically. The occasional male tortoiseshell is produced but they are always sterile owing to the peculiarities of the tortoiseshell gene—it is passed down the female line only.

The British Tortoiseshell isn't a modern breed and has been shown since the very beginning of cat shows. Despite its strange female-only genetic function it has survived extremely well by out-crossing with studs of black, red, or cream shorthairs. In the resulting litters should be some tortoiseshells and the rest good examples of the self-color of the stud cat.

The colors should be well mixed throughout the coat for the British Tortoiseshell Shorthair but for the Tortoiseshell-and-White (originally known as the Chintz) they should be clearly defined as patches of cream, black, red, and white. Other colors allowed include the Blue Tortoiseshell-and-White which is known as Dilute Calico in the US.

The British Tortoiseshell is a sturdy cat with a muscular, stocky body and conforms well to the British standard for shorthairs. It has a round broad head with a straight nose and medium-size ears that have round tips. The eyes are large, round, and should be bright orange (UK) or deep copper (US).

In the pure tortoiseshell the coat should be evenly patched with black, red, and cream, and a blaze of red or cream on the forehead is much preferred. In the Blue Tortoiseshell-and-White the red is replaced with cream and the black with blue. The nose leather should be pink or blue, or both.

This is an affectionate cat, known by many generations as "tortie," and it is good with children and extremely faithful. It is a home-loving cat with no bad features or characteristics. It has spent most of its life as a rough tough farm cat so it's a survivor but it does still appreciate a warm fireside and a comfortable lap upon which to curl. It has been called greedy by many owners but that might just be a throwback to lean times it may have experienced on farms in its early days.

Exotic Shorthair

Country of origin: USA

Type:
shorthaired Persian

Facial characteristics:
broad and large head with a short
snub nose and small ears; eyes
are large and round, and should
be bright copper (deep orange in
the UK) except for the Silvers
which should be hazel
(green in the UK)

Coat:
longer than a shorthair but not as
long as a longhair—plush, thick,
and dense

Color:
any as for Persians

Temperament:
gentle, docile, affectionate

Associated breeds:
other shorthairs and Persians

During the early development of many British shorthair breeds, color examples were taken from the Persian breeds to try to get the right colors for the shorthairs. But what often happened was that shorthaired Persians were produced instead. At first these were not wanted and the kittens were given away as pets. But during the early 1960s the potential was spotted and the breed given its own name—the Exotic Shorthair—and a type approval as well as recognition by the major cat associations. So here was a Persian without any of the problems of daily grooming. It is ideal for lazy people, busy people, and people with cat allergies who want a Persian but can't tolerate the hair. The Exotic Shorthair isn't quite as shorthaired as the British shorthaired varieties but it is still substantially shorter than a Persian.

It is a gentle placid cat which makes it ideal to show and have as a pet if you live in a flat or gardenless house. It enjoys being handled and petted immensely. The fur is best described as "plush" and benefits from being brushed tail to head which, although most cats hate this, the Exotic Shorthair actually enjoys. The fur can also be groomed by running a soft leather cloth over it.

The Exotic Shorthair is a medium to large cobby-build cat with a medium coat length of dense plush fur which is soft and stands well away from the body due to its density. It can be penalized as a show cat if the fur lies flat or close to the body. Its head is round and quite massive, with a large skull and a short thick neck. It has a round face with full cheeks and broad powerful jaws. Its chin is full and well developed. The eyes are large, round, and set quite far apart. They are usually copper or orange in the UK but eye color depends on the coat color and should always conform to it.

above: **Exotic Black Spotted
Silver Shorthair.**

right: **Exotic Cream Shorthair.**

below: **Exotic Blue Tabby Colorpoint Shorthair.**

Because the Exotic Shorthair inherited its broad face and tiny nose from its Persian ancestry it has a very cute-looking face, which endears it to the public and breeders alike, and it has become an extremely popular cat. It is very docile and sweet natured. Generally it is a very undemanding cat which is affectionate and loving.

All colors and color combinations that hold good for the Persian are accepted, including such exotic varieties as the Colorpoint Exotic and the Blue Tabby Exotic. Both of these are very popular. Most of the varieties of the Exotic Shorthair are still only available in the United States but the breed and its popularity is spreading worldwide.

American Wirehair

Country of origin: USA

Type:
American shorthair

Facial characteristics:
round head with a well-developed chin; medium-size nose; large round eyes of a brilliant golden color, and medium-size ear with rounded tips

Coat:
short and woolly

Color:
all as for other American shorthairs except chestnut brown (chocolate in the UK), lavender (lilac in the UK), colorpoints

Temperament:
gentle, affectionate, even-tempered

Associated breeds:
other American shorthairs

The latest addition to the American Shorthair breed is the American Wirehair which was the result of a natural "mutation" in 1966. In a litter of pedigree Red-and-White Shorthairs a wire or curly coated shorthair appeared. This was "Adam" and he became the first of what is now an immensely popular breed. It is named for the wire-haired terriers of the dog world because it was thought the coat had the same attributes. The Wirehair was given official status in 1977 and is now available in a variety of colors including all the usual for American Shorthairs. Its curly coat, which has the same feel and texture as that of a lamb, makes it very cuddly which may be why it has found such popularity especially with families who have small children. The wire coat is extremely easy to maintain and the wire gene is dominant which makes it extremely easy to breed true and to introduce other color variations. The only colors not approved of are any oriental colorpoints and chestnut brown (chocolate in the UK) or lavender (lilac in the UK). The Wirehair is a very even-tempered, well-adjusted cat which takes things in its stride. It is very affectionate and gentle.

Oriental and Foreign Shorthairs

Country of origin: USA, UK

Type:
oriental shorthair

Facial characteristics:
wedge-shaped, oriental-looking
head; almond-shaped slanted
eyes; large pointed ears

Coat:
short, fine textured,
close lying

Color:
white, black, blue, red, cream,
lavender (lilac in the UK), cameo,
silver, chestnut brown (chocolate
in the UK), cinnamon, caramel
brown (cinnamon in the UK),
black smoke, chestnut smoke,
cameo smoke, tabby,
and tortoiseshell

Temperament:
vocal, demanding, extremely
affectionate, loving

Associated breeds:
Siamese, other shorthairs

Oriental Shorthairs are all classed together under the one name in the United States, and then divided into five groups: shaded, solids, tabbies, smokes, and particolors. The last group is called bicolors in the UK. However, in the UK they use the term "foreign" to mean oriental-looking and each cat is given its own classification, such as Foreign Lavender, Foreign Tabby, and so on. This obviously leads to a great deal of confusion.

The breeding programs in the USA and the UK took a very similar line and came about for the same reason— breeders felt the need to develop a Siamese without colorpoints. They wanted a cat with a pure self-color but that retained all the characteristics of the Siamese. The first experiments were aimed at producing a completely brown cat with the oriental look. This was

achieved in both the United States and Britain by crossing sealpoint Siamese with Russian Blues. This is listed under Oriental Shorthairs as Brown Oriental Shorthair, but in the UK this cat is known as the Havana and warrants a separate breed class that is all its own.

During the 1960s, again on both sides of the Atlantic, new varieties of oriental shorthairs were produced. Recognition by the various cat associations was achieved in the 1970s, with class and breed standards being set.

Fewer colors are recognized in the USA than in the UK. Today nearly all colors and color combinations can be produced, resulting in some very exotic-looking oriental-type cats. The Oriental White was produced, for example, by crossing Siamese with white shorthairs. It is a stunning cat, with smooth fur and startling blue eyes. Also whereas most

right: **Cream Oriental.**

left: **Chocolate Tortie Silver Ticked Tabby Oriental.**

below: **Blue Oriental.**

blue-eyed white cats are deaf, the Oriental White has escaped this affliction. Blue-eyed cats are preferred throughout the whole range of oriental shorthairs in the UK but there is a less strict policy in the USA, and green and gold are allowed too.

Oriental Tabbies were produced by crossing non-pedigree tabbies with Siamese and then, once tabby-point Siamese had been produced, using them. The Oriental Lavender (Foreign Lilac in the UK) was produced by crossing British Havanas, which themselves were produced by crossing Russian Blues with Siamese sealpoints. In fact, in any litter with Havana parents, you always get a couple of Oriental Lavenders.

The colors usually seen are: white, black, blue, red, cream, lavender (lilac in the UK), cameo, silver, chestnut brown (chocolate in the UK), cinnamon, caramel brown (cinnamon in the UK), black smoke, chestnut smoke, cameo smoke, tabby, and tortoiseshell. The situation in the UK is further complicated by solid-color cats being known as Foreign Shorthairs while any shaded, ticked, or spotted cats are called Oriental Shorthairs. With luck this situation will be clarified and there will be a better definition which will be the same for the USA and the UK.

The cat looks and behaves like a Siamese but has a different color coat. The shorthaired Oriental or Foreign retains its vocal calling, its sense of fun, and its inquisitive and curious nature. It's a demanding cat and expects a lot of attention and shouldn't be left alone for too long. It is a very people-focused cat which makes its wishes known extremely well.

It is a medium-size cat with a long body, a wedge-shaped head, and a fine muzzle. It has large pointed ears and a long tapering tail. Its coat is short, tight, fine, and glossy. The coat is very easy to maintain because it doesn't need grooming but rather the occasional running over with a hand or silk scarf to keep the gloss at its highest.

Abyssinian

Country of origin: Abyssinia (now Ethiopia)

No one is entirely sure about the origin of the Abyssinian cat. Of the various theories, the most romantic is also the most likely. It is asserted that the Abyssinian was bred from cats imported to Britain in the middle of the nineteenth century from Abyssinia (now Ethiopia), which borders Egypt. These cats certainly bear a striking resemblance to the cats depicted in ancient Egyptian paintings and sculptures. It is therefore thought that the Abyssinian is the direct descendant of the sacred Egyptian cats, and is the oldest breed in the world.

The more prosaic view of the origins of the Abyssinian is that it was bred in the second half of the nineteenth century with the intention of creating a breed which looked like the original Egyptian cat. Since the Romans certainly brought cats to Britain from Egypt, the resident tabby cat population must have included the original Egyptian gene, so this version is scientifically plausible.

One of the most striking features of the Abyssinian is its ticked, or agouti, fur. This means that each hair has two or three darker bands along its length. Abyssinians were once known as rabbit or hare cats because of this ticking. Certainly the ticked fur makes Abyssinians one of the most individual and distinctive breeds of cat.

The original color Abyssinian is called the Ruddy (Usual in the UK) and was followed fairly swiftly by many other colors. The Ruddy is actually a reddish brown cat with black ticking. The other permitted colors are the

Type:
shorthaired oriental
(shorthaired foreign in the UK)

Facial characteristics:
round slightly wedge-shaped head
with large almond-shaped eyes
set wide apart

Coat:
soft, dense fur with two to three
bands of ticking

Color:
ruddy (Usual in the UK), sorrel,
blue, silver, chestnut brown
(chocolate in the UK), lavender
(lilac in the UK), fawn, red,
cream, tortie

Temperament:
varies—can be demanding, can
be sweet natured, but always
alert and intelligent

Associated breeds:
Somali

above: **Abyssinian Cat.**

Sorrel, which is a coppery red cat with chestnut brown (chocolate in the UK) ticking; the Blue, which is a warmish blue-gray cat with black-blue ticking; the Fawn, which is a fawn cat with darker fawn ticking; the Lavender (Lilac in the UK) which is a pinkish-gray cat with darker lavender ticking; the Silver, which is a silver cat with black ticking; the Silver Sorrel, which is a peach-silver cat with chestnut brown ticking, and the Silver Blue, which is a silvery blue-gray cat with a deep blue ticking.

The head is round and softly wedge shaped, with a medium to large nose. The eyes are large and almond shaped, and permitted eye colors are hazel, amber, and green depending on coat color. The coat is glossy and soft to the touch but it is also dense and quite long. The body is quite long and extremely muscular looking. The legs are very long and slender and give the cat the appearance of standing on tiptoe. The paw pads should be black. Nose

leather should be brick red. The tail is long and tapering and should be tipped with the ticking color. The Abyssinian's nature is controversial—some say it is a sweet-natured gentle cat while others find it extremely bad tempered and aggressive. Some say it is obedient, others that it is wilful. Some owners say they have never had such an intelligent cat while others report quite the opposite.

above: **Fawn Abyssinian.**

left: **Blue Abyssinian.**

Bengal

Country of origin: USA

To understand why the Bengal is such a fantastic cat both in looks and its unusual breeding we have to know a little of its ancestry. One cross was the tabby, and we are familiar with that, but the other cross was the leopard cat of Asia. It is no domestic mix but a real wildcat in every sense of the word.

The leopard cat is very adaptable and is found throughout southeast Asia as well as far north into Siberia. It has even been found on some of the Philippine Islands and Bali. It is a solitary animal except at breeding times when several males will gather together to court the same female. An average litter is only three kittens. The leopard cat likes to live close to human habitation and has been known to be very fond of taking chickens.

The cross of a leopard cat with a tabby created a very wild-looking cat but with the gentle temperament of the domestic shorthair. The coat is short to medium and very silky and soft. It is a thick coat though and the color is a very soft creamy orange with rosettes of darker patches of color from red to black. The eyes are large, round, and a pale greeny orange. The ears are large and pointed, and the head should be large with a short nose. This cat doesn't have any trace of the Siamese look but rather looks like a very sleek domestic shorthair with, of course, this wild-looking leopard coat. It is a truly beautiful cat. Its temperament is extremely loving and affectionate, and it has a curious call, not unlike a bird chirrup, which is quite unlike that of any other cat—and it will call a lot to

its owner. The Bengal name was chosen to represent the sort of location you would expect to see this cat if it wasn't quite so at home in the United States, and there are still very few examples about. At the last count just over two hundred cats were listed with the cat associations in the USA.

Since its first inception the Bengal has grown rapidly in popularity and the range of colors has now been extended. It includes the Brown Tabby Bengal, which has deep reddish brown spots on a golden coat with deep golden eyes and black paw pads. Also there is the Blue-Eyed Snow Bengal, which—as its name suggests—is a blue-eyed variety with its spots restricted to the conventional colorpoint locations of a Siamese, although there is still a very faint patterning over the whole pale cream body.

Finally the Marble Bengal has striking markings with a marble pattern of whorls, streaks, swirls, spots, and curvy lines.

Type:
shorthair

Facial characteristics:
large head with short nose; large round eyes; large pointed ears

Coat:
short to medium in length with a silky soft feel and very thick

Color:
spotted, marbled, brown, and blue

Temperament:
gentle, affectionate, vocal

Associated breeds:
other American shorthairs

below: **Snow Bengal.**

Bombay

Countries of origin: USA and UK, but independently and producing separate cats

Type:
shorthair, oriental type

Facial characteristics:
USA sleek, UK rounder

Coat:
short

Color:
black only

Temperament:
USA very affectionate and demanding; UK more independent but still very affectionate

Associated breeds:
other shorthairs, Burmese

Because of the difference in standards between the USA and the UK there is sometimes confusion as to what a cat is called, its characteristics, and even its ancestry. The Bombay is one of those cats. In the United States the Bombay is a sleek black cat bred by crossing black American shorthairs with sable Burmese. In the UK the Bombay is a fatter cat altogether, produced by crossing black British shorthairs with Burmese, and this cat is known as the Black Asian by Americans.

The American Bombay was so called because it closely resembles a miniature version of the black Asian leopard. It is not recognized in the UK. Both versions are bred, recognized, and accepted in the USA as both the Bombay and the Black Asian.

The American Bombay is a jet black slinky cat with golden eyes and a short close-lying coat of extremely silky fur. Its paw pads should be black, as should its nose leather. The tail is long, tapering, and quite thick at the base. It has a wedge-shaped head with large round eyes. It is happy to spend its entire life indoors and craves human company almost more than a Siamese. It constantly purrs and is very affectionate and loving. This is an extremely elegant and sleek cat with a very glossy coat and a certain oriental appearance.

The American Black Asian (the British Bombay) is a more solid cat with a stockier body. It is not nearly as sleek or slinky as the American Bombay. It is rounder, more muscular, and more cobby; and the fur is slightly longer and fluffier. It should have black paw pads and nose leather but a rounder head, and smaller ears which are more rounded than its American cousin. Its paws are more rounded whereas the American Bombay has more oval paws. The eye color is more copper than gold. The American Black Asian is also more independent, less vocal, and less demanding of human attention and company.

Both cats should not have white fur or tabby markings showing, although any kitten may have faint markings which will fade by the time it is six months old. Both cats should have long straight tails with no kinks.

right: **Black Bombay.**

Burmese

Country of origin: Burma

Type:
medium size, sturdy but elegant; long, slim legs; small oval paws with pads which match the coat color

Facial characteristics:
medium wedge-shaped head with a shortish nose; medium-size, wide-set ears, with slightly rounded tips; round or oval, slightly slanted eyes, yellow to gold in color

Coat:
short, close-lying, and very glossy fur

Color:
originally brown, but other varieties now include blue, chestnut brown (chocolate in the UK), lavender (lilac in the UK), red, cream, brown tortie, chestnut brown tortie, lavender tortie

Temperament:
very affectionate, intelligent, extrovert, with a sense of humor, and great ingenuity

Associated breeds:
Tonkinese, Bombay, Tiffanie

As far back as the fifteenth century, brown cats known as *rajahs* lived in the Buddhist temples of Burma. These were the forerunners of the modern Burmese cat, which is growing in popularity so fast it may soon outstrip the Siamese.

All Burmese cats in the West can trace their ancestry back to a female called Wong Mau who was brought to California from Burma in 1930, and crossed with a Siamese. Within a few generations, and with a few more cats from Burma introduced to prevent inbreeding, the modern Burmese cat was established. The first Burmese were sable, or brown, in color.

Since then, the breed has developed and many new colors have been introduced. The American and British standards for the breed differ: The American Burmese is rounded and sturdy, while the British Burmese is quite oriental in appearance. For the first twenty-odd years, all Burmese cats were brown, but in 1955, two brown Burmese parents surprised their owners by producing a blue kitten. Since then many other colors have been bred; first chestnut brown (chocolate in the UK) and lavender (lilac in the UK), followed by a range of other variations. Although there are many differences and variations in coloring there does seem to be a consensus of opinion about the temperament of the Burmese.

They are not as vocal nor as highly strung as the Siamese and are considered to be very adaptable, good hunters, charming, and humorous, as well as being boisterous and extremely affectionate. The females mature early, coming into heat at about seven months and, if allowed to mate, will produce about five kittens. They are a long-lived cat—around 16 to 18 years—but there is a tendency toward deformed kittens owing to rather high inbreeding over the years which causes congenital skeletal abnormalities.

The Bombay is also known as the mini-panther and is, naturally, completely black. They are, however, not black Burmese but now recognized as a separate breed produced by mating a brown Burmese with a black American Shorthair in the United States in 1958. They have copper-colored eyes.

left: **Brown Burmese.**

below: **Chocolate Burmese.**

Burmilla

Country of origin: UK

Type:
oriental shorthair

Facial characteristics:
round head, large green eyes;
brick-red nose leather
with black rim

Coat:
short but dense and soft

Color:
silver tipped only

Temperament:
gentle, affectionate,
even-tempered

Associated breeds:
Burmese, Chinchilla,
other shorthairs

The Burmilla is the result of crossing a Burmese with a Chinchilla. It is a beautiful cat with a silver-tipped coat and a Burmese-type body. It was developed in the UK during the 1980s by an accidental mating of a Lavender Burmese with a Chinchilla stud at the cattery owned by the Baroness von Kirchberg. Four kittens were born and these became the breeding stock for the future Burmilla. Curiously it isn't yet recognized in the UK as a separate breed but is accepted in the United States.

This is an exceptionally striking cat with short fur that is longer than its Burmese ancestry but still very dense and extremely soft. The body shape, like the Burmese, is lithe and muscular. It should have a rounded head and a short nose, with a brick-red nose pad rimmed in black. There should be a faint "M" tabby marking on the forehead and the ears are quite large and rounded at the tips.

right: **Blue shaded Burmilla.**

Egyptian Mau

Countries of origin: Italy, Egypt, USA

Type:
oriental shorthair

Facial characteristics:
wedge-shaped; pale-green
almond-shaped eyes; scarab
marking on the forehead

Coat:
silky, medium to short, dense

Color:
silver, bronze, pewter, smoke,
and black

Temperament:
playful, loving,
affectionate, intelligent

Associated breeds:
other shorthairs

No one is quite sure of the origins of the Egyptian Mau. What we know is that one appeared at a cat show in Milan in 1953 and again in Rome in the mid 1950s but its ancestry is unclear. It may well be a genuine breed imported from Cairo as there are similar cats there, or it may have been bred "artificially" by an Italian breeder.

In the UK a similar result was achieved by producing spotted Siamese-type cats. Their version was originally called the Mau but the name has now been changed to the Oriental Spotted Longhair, and the American Egyptian Mau is not accepted or recognized in the UK by the cat associations.

The US version—the Egyptian Mau—is a strikingly beautiful cat with fine silky fur that is quite dense and medium length. It is a very adaptable cat which is said to be fond of learning tricks and is one of the very few cats which will take to walking on a lead.

right: **Silver Egyptian Mau.**

Havana Brown

Country of origin: UK and USA independently

Type:
shorthaired, oriental type

Facial characteristics:
UK oriental, USA rounder—
both green eyes

Coat:
short-haired, sleek, glossy

Color:
warm brown only

Temperament:
UK same as for Siamese;
US more like that of the
Russian Blue

Associated breeds:
UK Siamese; USA other shorthairs

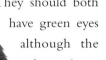

Again we have two cats which are independently recognized in the USA and the UK but share the same name and have similar, though slightly different, characteristics. In the UK the Havana was developed by crossing sealpoint Siamese with a shorthaired black which itself had Siamese origins. The breed was successfully accepted by the cat associations in the UK by 1958 and has continued to go from strength to strength. Occasional out-crosses to Siamese keep the breed healthy and fresh.

In the USA it was decided to use oriental-type shorthairs other than Siamese, and to produce a slightly less oriental-looking cat called the Havana Brown. The American version is a sturdy cat with a more muscular body and a rounder face. Because it doesn't have quite the concentrated Siamese ancestry it tends to be less vocal and less demanding—indeed it is quite a bit more independent.

The USA Havana is more of a chestnut brown, whereas its British counterpart is a darker richer brown color. They should both have green eyes although the American version has rounder eyes whereas the UK version has almond-shaped eyes.

Just to complicate things, there is another version in the USA which corresponds much more closely to the UK Havana—the American Oriental Self Brown, which is very similar in shape, size, coloring, and ancestry to the British Havana.

The name Havana was chosen to represent the color—it is supposed to be the rich brown of a very good Cuban cigar although there are those in Britain who say it is named after the Havana rabbit which was bred in the UK during the 1950s. Whatever its source, the cat should still be the color of a good cigar.

In the UK the standard for judging the Havana is the same as for the Siamese, whereas the standards in the USA are the same as for the Russian Blue.

The interesting thing is that there was originally a genuine all-brown Siamese that was imported into the UK as long ago as 1888 when it was shown at the Crystal Palace Cat Show in London and won first prize. This breed was still around in the 1920s because we know one such cat won a special prize at a Siamese Cat Show for "best chocolate body." But these brown Siamese cats—and we don't know how many or how popular they were—had what was deemed a fault: they were green eyed. Thus the poor brown Siamese fell into disuse and vanished, and it had to wait nearly 40 years to be re-created in the UK. It was probably the arrival of the Burmese that set breeders thinking about the possibilities of a brown Siamese again.

Japanese Bobtail

Country of origin: Japan

Type:
shorthaired

Facial characteristics:
wedge-shaped head with large round eyes which appear slanted when seen from the side; eye color should conform to coat color

Coat:
short and fine

Color:
any except Siamese colorpoints; traditionally in Japan only tricolor (black, red, and white) and tortoiseshell-and-white

Temperament:
friendly, playful, full of character

Associated breeds:
none

above: **Blue-eyed Japanese Bobtail.**

Many people think the Japanese Bobtail is a created breed. However, in fact this is one of the oldest breeds we know. It is genuinely Japanese in origin and is the national cat of Japan where it is known as the *maneki-neko,* which means the "beckoning" cat. And that's exactly what the Japanese Bobtail seems to do; it lifts one paw in a curious gesture which, in Japan, is said to bring good luck.

In Japan the Japanese Bobtail is found in only two varieties—the tricolor and the tortoiseshell-and-white—but in the USA, where this cat has found quite some popularity since it was imported in the 1960s, it is accepted in a wide range of colors except Siamese color-points.

The bobtail is exactly what it has—a little bobbed tail much like a rabbit's—and it's completely natural.

Korat

Country of origin: Thailand (formerly Siam)

Type:
oriental shorthair

Facial characteristics:
round, heart-shaped face;
green eyes; large ears

Coat:
short, soft, silky

Color:
only silver-blue

Temperament:
affectionate, very loving,
good with children

Associated breeds:
none

Although only fairly recently accepted by cat associations—1966 in the USA and 1975 in the UK—this is a very ancient breed that has been known about and shown for some considerable time. It is a native of Thailand (which used to be called Siam) where it comes from the Korat province—hence the name. But in Thailand it is known as the *si-sawat*, which means cat of great good fortune. A si-sawat is also a Thai fruit with silver-blue seeds which is the color of the Korat's fur.

They were first shown in the UK in 1896 as Blue Siamese but failed dismally as they aren't blue but a rather beautiful silver-blue (or biscuit as some call it). The other problem was that nobody could buy a Korat. They are so special in Thailand that you can only acquire one by being given it. There is simply no other way because they were reserved for royalty only. Even today ownership of a Korat in Thailand is restricted by government regulations.

In the USA where they are now bred (as well as the UK), you can acquire one easily—if you can afford it. It is a lovely cat with a charming and fiercely loyal temperament. They don't like other cats though and can be quite aggressive toward them, especially males.

below: **Silver Blue Korat.**

Manx

Country of origin: UK (Isle of Man)

The Isle of Man lies off the northwest coast of England and this is where the Manx cat developed, in isolation from the rest of the world. The cat got there either by being washed ashore from England or by being taken by early sailors, although some say it was an oriental cat washed ashore from a sinking Spanish ship at the time of the Armada.

The reason it appears not to have a tail is because it carries a defective tail gene which causes it to have skeletal deformity (unlike the Japanese Bobtail (see page 202) which carries a recessive gene). The Isle of Man is quite flat and doesn't require great climbing abilities which tailless cats do not have. Even so the Manx has adapted by developing longer back legs than its front ones, which allow it to balance extremely well. It also has very muscular back thighs which help it considerably.

In fact the Manx does have a tail and its length depends on what sort of Manx it is, as there are four.

All four types are accepted and recognized as true Manx cats but only the Rumpies can be shown at cat shows. The other three groups are important because they are used for breeding purposes. If you breed two Rumpies, the result is dead kittens because the defective gene leads to fatal deformities.

In the UK a Manx club has been in existence since 1901. The cat was imported into the USA in the 1930s and was immediately given recognition. It is the mascot cat of the Isle of Man and appears on their coins.

The Manx has a double coat of plush fur with a thinner undercoat. All colors are allowed and the desired body shape is rounded with an arched or curved back although in the United States the longer back legs are penalized at shows. It's a friendly cat with a great love of swimming, and it makes a very good pet.

above: **Brown Patched Classic Manx.**

right: **Red Spotted Manx.**

Type:
tailless shorthair

Facial characteristics:
rounded; eye color to conform to coat color, medium-size ears

Coat:
short, double, plush, thick

Color:
virtually any but especially solid, bicolor, tabby, calico, marbled, and tortie

Temperament:
friendly, independent, good natured, family orientated

Associated breeds:
other shorthairs

THE RUMPY
this cat has genuinely no visible tail, and may actually display a small hollow where the tail would have been

THE RUMPY-RISER
this has a little knob of a tail externally, and internally a few tail vertebrae

THE STUMPY
this cat has a short tail which invariably is curved or kinked, and is usually movable

THE LONGIE
this cat has a tail which is only slightly shorter than a normal cat's

Ocicat

Country of origin: USA

The American Ocicat is a well-documented breed—we even know the name of the very first one: Tong. It reminded its breeder of a baby ocelot when it was first born—hence the name. It was produced by crossing a half-Siamese, half-Abyssinian queen with a chocolate-point Siamese. The resulting kittens were tabby and began the breed, which was accepted for recognition in the 1960s. Since then the breed has been helped by the introduction of breeding stock from American Shorthairs and three breeds—Abyssinian, Siamese, and American Shorthairs—are now regularly used to keep the breed fresh and genetically "clean."

The male Ocicat is a very large cat and can weigh over 15 pounds, whereas the female is a medium-size cat. They are muscular, with well-proportioned heads, large pricked ears, and long tapering tails. The main colors are a tawny buff with black or brown spots, and the polka-dotted version also comes in silver with black spots. There is also a blue, a bronze, a sienna, a chestnut brown, and a lavender. The eye color should conform to the coat, with a range from green to copper. This is a fun-loving friendly cat which is very good with children and adores being pampered.

Type:
oriental shorthair

Facial characteristics:
wedge-shaped head with a broad muzzle and short nose

Coat:
short with glossy close-lying fur; ticked with at least two colors

Color:
tawny, silver, blue, lavender, golden, chestnut brown, sienna

Temperament:
fun loving, friendly, with a dog-like devotion to its owner

Associated breeds:
Siamese, Abyssinian, American shorthairs

left: **Silver Spotted Ocicat.**

Cornish Rex and Devon Rex

Country of origin: UK

Type:
curly shorthair

Facial characteristics:
oriental type—more so in the
Devon Rex; curly eyebrows
and whiskers

Coat:
curly thin fur

Color:
any

Temperament:
inquisitive, friendly,
talkative, independent

Associated breeds:
other shorthairs, Siamese

The Rex cat is formed by a recessive gene mutation which produces a curly fur and is usually only found in rabbits (the Rex rabbit is so named because of the gene and that's where the name for the Rex cat comes from). It first appeared in one kitten in a litter of farm cats in Cornwall, England, in 1950. The owner bred the kitten back to its mother and the subsequent kittens all had the curly coat (and the recessive gene).

A similar kitten was found in Devon, England, in 1960 and was bred back to its mother. However if you put the two together the curly coat vanishes and you only get straight-coated kittens because the two varieties are caused by different recessive genes and are not compatible.

The fur is very fine and they rarely shed which makes them susceptible to extremes of temperature so they have to be protected. Nevertheless they make good pets and they are very sociable. They are now available in virtually all colors as for other shorthairs and there is now even a Rex with Siamese colorpoints—the Si-Rex.

below: **Black Smoke Devon Rex.**

left: **Cornish Rex.**

Russian Blue

Country of origin: originally Russia

The Russian Blue is a handsome and unique cat. It is a completely natural breed and not the result of genetic modification of any sort, but it has undergone some changes—such as in eye color. The first Russian Blues were imported into the West from the White Sea port of Archangel which is just outside the Arctic Circle. It was brought to England by Russian sailors during the latter part of the nineteenth century and was used for bartering and trading. Russian Blues were shown widely at cat shows in England during the 1890s when they had bright orange eyes which subsequently have been changed to green.

During World War II the Russian Blue went into something of a decline, as did many breeds in the UK, and afterward the breed became very altered by cross-breeding with Siamese. This was a disaster and new original stock had to be imported, especially from Sweden, to re-establish the correct standard. Today the Russian Blue is a fine example of the original type with no trace of Siamese in it.

Going back to its origins, it was first called the Archangel cat for its place of export and has been called the Spanish Blue, the Maltese Blue, and even the American Blue. Probably the most famous example of this breed was the cat, Vashka, which was owned by Tsar Nicholas II of Russia.

Russian Blues are quite a challenge to breed because they are a complex cat— you get the coat color right only to find the body shape is too oriental; or you get the body shape right only to find the eye color is wrong; or you get all those right only to find that you've missed the silver-tipped guard hairs. Other difficulties include fur that is too thin, ears that are too small, the nose pad not being blue, paw pads not being pinky mauve (blue in the UK), or front legs that are not short enough (they should be shorter than the hind legs). It is a very difficult business breeding a perfect Russian Blue which is why the breed—despite its enormous popularity—is still extremely rare and expensive.

The only color permitted in both the USA and the UK is the blue. However in New Zealand an all-black version and an all-white version have been bred but so far have not been recognized or accepted outside the country.

The Russian Blue may suffer from too much heat in some parts of North America but it is very adept at staying warm so it has no problems in the UK and northern Canada. It can also lose its thickness of coat and turn a much paler color if kept in too warm an environment.

It is an intelligent and serene cat which doesn't like loud noises or too many disturbances, so is not a good cat to have around children. It makes a shy and retiring pet but is extremely loving and pleasant to be with.

Type:
shorthair, medium oriental type

Facial characteristics:
wedge-shaped; large ears; green eyed

Coat:
short, silky fur

Color:
blue only

Temperament:
shy, gentle, serene, peace-loving

Associated breeds:
none

Scottish Fold

Country of origin: Scotland

Type:
shorthaired, folded ear

Facial characteristics:
broad face; large green eyes;
folded ears

Coat:
short dense fur

Color:
originally only white; now black,
blue, red, tabby, cream,
smoke, chinchilla

Temperament:
friendly but dedicated to one
person exclusively

Associated breeds:
other shorthairs

top: **Black and White Scottish Fold.**

below: **Calico Scottish Fold.**

The most obvious feature about the Scottish Fold is that its ears are folded forward, making the cat look as if it is wearing a cap—or has recently been wearing one. Legend has it that the original Fold cat was brought to England in the 1880s by sailors returning from China. Never before had a non-erect-eared cat been seen so it caused quite a stir when exhibited. It wasn't taken too seriously though and the breed vanished only to reappear in 1961 in farm cats in Perthshire, Scotland.

It isn't known whether these cats are descendants of the original Chinese cats from the nineteenth century or not. This breed is recognized and accepted in the USA but not in the UK or Europe where it is felt the folded ears are detrimental to the cat and would encourage ear mites and faulty hearing. The gene which causes the folded ear is, however, also responsible for an abnormality which causes a thickening in the rear legs and tail. Originally this was considered desirable but as it interferes with the cat's walking ability it is now being bred out as much as possible. The Scottish Fold has a wide head with a short neck, round orange eyes, a large nose, and short dense fur. It is friendly although it is predominantly a one-person cat.

Siamese

Country of origin: Thailand (formerly Siam)

The history of the Siamese is authenticated as far back as the fourteenth century. The Siamese cat was a popular and well-loved breed in the city of Ayudha in Siam (now Thailand), which was founded in 1350 and was the capital city for over four hundred years. The Siamese cat features in the manuscript known as the *Cat-Book Poems*, an entire book of pictures and poems devoted to the cat, written in Siam between 1350 and 1750. Although the Siamese cat was not the only native breed in Siam, it seems to have been the most popular, and was the breed which was kept in the royal palaces.

When the Siamese cat first arrived in the West, in the second half of the nineteenth century, it had two genetic defects in particular which breeders are still trying hard to eliminate. One of these was a noticeable squint and the other was a kink in the tail. The cats, however, brought with them several delightful explanations for these features. One reason for the kink was said to be that the cats' tails were used by the royalty of Siam for looking after their rings; they developed the kink to stop the rings falling off. Another explanation for both features was that the temple cats of Siam were put in charge of guarding an extremely valuable vase. They took their job very seriously and wrapped their tails tightly round the vase, staring at it so intently that they went cross-eyed.

The King of Siam helped make the cat popular. In the 1880s he gave two Siamese cats to Owen Gould who was then the British consul general in Bangkok. Owen Gould brought them back to London with him and showed them at the Crystal Palace Cat Show in London. By 1890 Siamese cats had made it to America by way of being a gift from the King of Siam to an American friend. This man showed them and within a few years they were being bred in the USA—and commanding very high prices, around $1,000 a kitten.

Partly because of its playful character and vocal attributes the Siamese was very popular during the 1920s—as indeed it still is—and breeders were hard pressed to keep up with the demand for these delightful oriental pets. This led to them taking short cuts which caused defects and faults, and very nearly led to the breed being wiped out. The breed recovered, though, but was again under severe threat in the 1960s and 1970s from another enemy—this time the feline leukemia virus.

Since then the Siamese has recovered and has now evolved into the sleek and graceful cat we all know. But it wasn't quite like that to start with. The original cats that came from Siam were much fatter and stockier than the Siamese we know today. They were nowhere near as sleek and slinky, and the heavily oriental appearance has been modified and altered to make

Type:
medium size, long, slim, athletic, with a long, thin tail

Facial characteristics:
long, wedge-shaped head; large pointed ears; almond-shaped blue eyes

Coat:
short, fine, close-lying fur

Temperament:
extrovert, intelligent, and lively, with a loud voice

Associated breeds:
Orientals, Angora, Balinese, Colorpoint shorthair (USA)

right: **Lilac Point Siamese.**

above: **Seal Point Siamese.**

the cat seem even more foreign and mysterious than it ever was in Siam. In fact the first standard for the cat, written in 1892, describes it as "a weighty but medium-size cat but not showing bulk." Gradually the wedge-shaped face has become even more marked, whereas the original Siamese cats had a very round face. In photographs from the late 1890s, Siamese look pretty much like a British shorthair but with colorpoints.

Siamese cats are one of the most popular breeds, if not *the* most popular of all. Both their looks and their temperament contribute to their popularity. They are among the most elegant of cats, with their long, slim bodies, long legs, and dainty feet. The colorpoint markings

VARIETY	COAT COLOR	MARKINGS
Seal-point	Cream	Seal brown
Blue-point	Bluish white	Gray-blue
Chestnut-brown-point	Ivory	Pale chestnut brown
Lavender-point	Magnolia	Pinkish-gray
Red-point	White shading to pale apricot	Reddish-gold
Cream-point	White shading to pale cream	Cream
Tabby-point	White	Tabby
Tortie-point	White	Tortoiseshell

only serve to highlight their regal appearance. The Siamese cat's large ears and long face are set off by wonderfully piercing blue eyes.

The temperament of the Siamese is as distinctive as its looks. They are very intelligent and extroverted, and often make devoted pets. But they can be imperious in their demands, and their loud voice makes them hard to ignore. They are the perfect example of the arrogant, inscrutable cat—but they are endearing nevertheless.

Siamese cats come in four main varieties, all colorpointed: seal-point, blue-point, chestnut-brown-point, and lavender-point. However, many other variations have since been bred. The first variety to be recognized as a breed was the seal-point. This cat is genetically black, but the pigment has been diluted and is restricted to the extremities of the head, legs, and tail. The table below shows the main varieties of Siamese cats, and indicates both the base coat color and the colorpoint markings. The first four listed are accepted in the United States. All of them are accepted in the UK, where all shorthaired color-pointed cats of oriental appearance are registered as Siamese whereas in the US only the four original colors of seal point, blue point, chocolate point and lilac point are accepted. Any of the red variations or the tabby (which is known as lynx-point in the US) are categorized as Colorpoint Shorthairs.

Technically the situation in the US may be correct as the Colorpoint Shorthairs are genetically not entirely Siamese. They were produced by mating Siamese with tabby shorthairs in order to achieve the new colors. However the gene which produces the colorpoints is recessive and the resulting kittens were colored all over. By mating these cross-bred cats back to high quality Siamese the correctly colorpointed kittens were produced. Successive crossing back has led to stable variations which now breed like-to-like. These new color variations have been accepted in the UK as real Siamese but not yet in the US.

Whatever colorpoint, whatever country it is bred in, whatever its ancestry and genetic inheritance, the Siamese still makes a delightful pet and companion with its vocal cry and playful nature.

Singapura

Countries of origin: Singapore, USA

Type:
shorthaired, oriental

Facial characteristics:
round face with a short muzzle,
very large eyes, pointed ears

Coat:
short, smooth, close lying

Color:
ivory with dark brown ticking—
Sepia Agouti

Temperament:
friendly but cautious

Associated breeds:
none

The Singapura is a genuine breed from Singapore which was first spotted for its potential by a breeder from America, Tommy Meadows.

In the mid 1970s she brought back a breeding pair of these strange and delightfully oriental cats and drew up a detailed and comprehensive breeding program which she stuck to, and the result speaks for itself. In Singapore the Singapura is a street cat of some character. It is a tough little cat with a very friendly but cautious nature. When they get to know you, they can be very affectionate.

They have a very short coat of fine ticked hair made up of bands of dark and light. The basic color is warm ivory with dark brown ticking. The color is known as Sepia Agouti. The muzzle, chin, chest, and stomach should be the color of unbleached cheesecloth, and only the body fur and tail are ticked. The eyes are hazel green or gold. The breed is still recent so comparatively rare.

below: **Brown Ticked Singapura.**

Snowshoe

Country of origin: USA

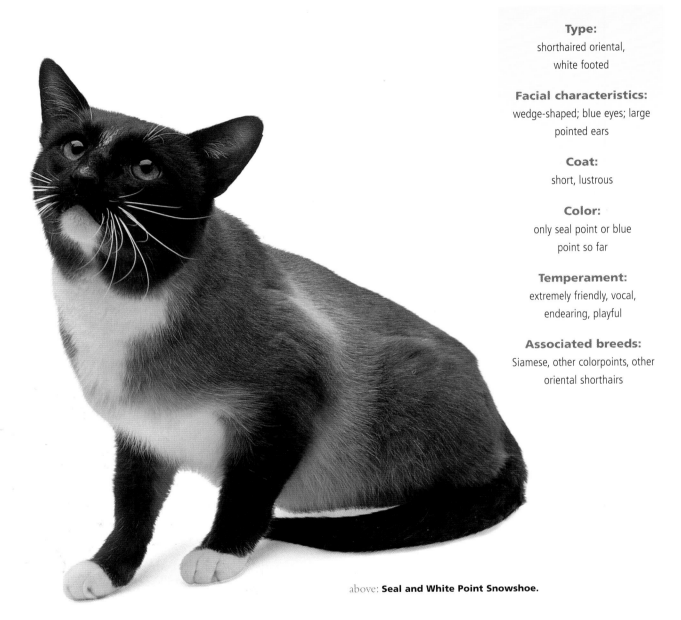

Type:
shorthaired oriental,
white footed

Facial characteristics:
wedge-shaped; blue eyes; large
pointed ears

Coat:
short, lustrous

Color:
only seal point or blue
point so far

Temperament:
extremely friendly, vocal,
endearing, playful

Associated breeds:
Siamese, other colorpoints, other
oriental shorthairs

above: **Seal and White Point Snowshoe.**

The Snowshoe looks just as if it is wearing tiny snowshoes. It is a modern bred cat, developed from the mating of two Siamese cats in the mid 1960s. In the resulting litter were three female kittens who carried the white feet. And that could have been the end of it without the clever intervention of some American breeders. They spotted the potential and began their breeding program by crossing some American Bicolor Shorthairs with the original three females. The first litters were registered as "Snowshoes" but were solid in color or bicolored. Any white-footed bicolors from that breeding were then crossed with Siamese to produce colorpointed and bicolor kittens. The resulting white-footed cats were then crossed with other colorpointed cats with white feet to produce the first true Snowshoes. These in turn were bred like-to-like and the breed now produces correctly every time with no throwbacks.

The Snowshoe is very much a people-focused cat and it loves attention. It is playful and needs a lot of company. It is still very rare.

Sphynx

Countries of origin: US, Canada

Type:
hairless, oriental

Facial characteristics:
wedge-shaped face; very large
ears; gold eyes; black nose

Coat:
none

Color:
all colors and patterns are
accepted if recognized
(they are discernable in the
vestigial coat and the skin)

Temperament:
extremely attention seeking,
prone to ailments

Associated breeds:
other oriental shorthairs

There are some people who call the Sphynx "the ugliest cat alive," but there are an equal number who really adore it. It first appeared in litters of American Shorthairs as a genetic mutation, and the Canadian breeders spotted the potential—hence its nickname, the Canadian Hairless—and developed the breed in the mid 1960s. Their efforts were not rewarded particularly with a very fertile cat nor a very robust one. The Sphynx doesn't breed true and hasn't been recognized or accepted by many of the larger cat associations. It is genuinely hairless but it constantly has to be crossed back to American Shorthairs. It is still the rarest cat on the planet and may well be the most expensive.

It has a tough wrinkled skin, enormous ears, and a very endearing look on its face. Its back is long and humped, it has very long legs for its size, and a long thin tail. The eyes are golden although a green-eyed version has been produced.

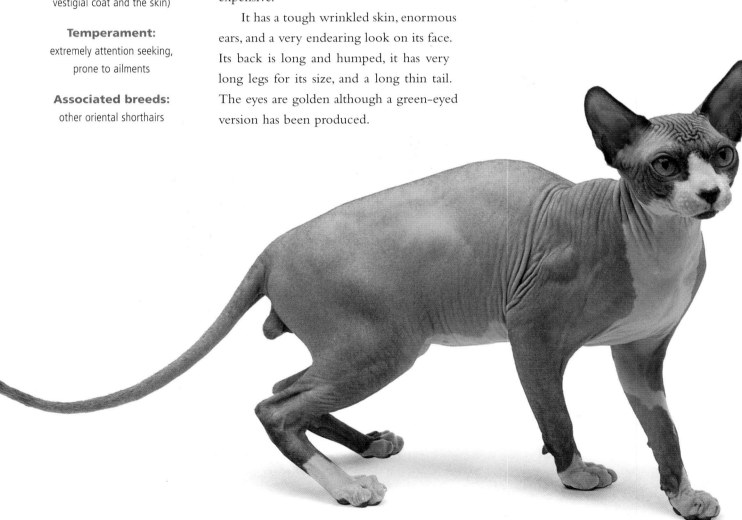

Tonkinese

Country of origin: USA

The Tonkinese is another artificially created pedigree but one which satisfies the finer points of both breeds from which it is drawn. It was produced during the 1960s by crossing Burmese with Siamese, and the result is a dark–coated Siamese with clearly defined colorpoints in the same color as the coat but much darker. Somehow the end result is a very satisfactory cat with a marvelous coat and a nice personality. The Tonkinese became accepted and recognized by all the major cat associations during the 1970s and 1980s, and today it is a popular and very individual cat.

When two Tonkinese are mated, the result is a litter made up of one half pure Tonkinese, one quarter pure Siamese, and one quarter pure Burmese. The Tonkinese has a coat that can only be described as luscious with a mink-like quality. This quality is reflected in the names given to the colors allowed— honey mink, natural mink, champagne mink, blue mink, platinum mink. All colors have pale blue eyes.

The Tonkinese temperament is friendly and extremely playful, but it is a ferocious hunter and will quickly and daringly remove any other small pets such as birds or rodents no matter how safe you think they are.

left: **Champagne Tonkinese.**

below: **Tonkinese.**

Type:
shorthaired oriental

Facial characteristics:
triangular with wide-set blue eyes and large rounded ears

Coat:
very dense, mink-like, luscious

Color:
honey mink, natural mink, blue mink, platinum mink, champagne mink

Temperament:
extremely lively, friendly, attentive, curious, ferocious hunter

Associated breeds:
Burmese, Siamese

Non-pedigree cats
Non-pedigree longhair

Countries of origin: Persia (now Iran), Turkey

Type:
longhaired, non-pedigree

Facial characteristics:
round head with large round eyes;
round-tipped ears

Coat:
longhaired with thick
silky fur

Color:
any, but mostly tabby—rarely
with colorpoints

Temperament:
calm, affectionate, easy

Associated breeds:
other longhaired cats, especially
Persians and Turkish

Many cat owners have beautiful and unusual cats and they often ask if they are a particular breed or whether they have a pedigree. Unfortunately they probably do not. There are an awful lot of non-pedigree longhaired cats who have made their way into the domestic home as pets. They are probably the result of show Persians and Turkish cats either escaping or producing sub-standard kittens which are then given away as pets and who themselves, when the time comes, breed with other domestic pets and perpetuate the non-pedigree line. Longhaired cats themselves are obviously Nature's way of making sure a cat doesn't get too cold when living in inhospitable circumstances—and both Persia (now Iran) and Turkey can get pretty cold in the winter.

If you look at the gene patterns of cats you will notice one quality which seems, and is, dominant—the tabby markings. Thus most "wild" longhaired non-pedigree cats will carry tabby markings. You may not be able to see them but they are there hidden in the long fur nevertheless.

The longhaired non-pedigree is usually a delightful pet; it is calmer and less demanding than its shorthaired cousin. It does, however, require more grooming.

below: **Long-haired Tabby and White cat.**

Non-pedigree tabby shorthair

Country of origin: worldwide

Forget all the pedigree cats, ignore the Persians, disregard the Siamese, and blank out the modern genetic breeds. It's the non-pedigree tabby shorthair that is going to rule the world.

This is the cat that's got the lot—dominant genes that is. There are two major ones in the cat world—the tabby gene and the shorthair gene. Thus the shorthaired tabby is ideal for a world where camouflage is essential and having a short coat is extremely helpful.

The tabby shorthair is friendly but independent, a good mouser and a fireside companion, and self-sufficient but loving. It won't run up too many vet's bills because it looks after itself extremely well, and it'll keep your home free of rodents.

Type:
shorthaired, non-pedigree

Facial characteristics:
broad round head with a short straight nose, large round eyes, usually green with black rims, and pink nose pad rimmed with black

Coat:
short, dense, soft

Colors:
tabby

Temperament:
gentle, easy, loving, independent

Associated breeds:
virtually all other shorthaired pedigrees owe something to this feline

left: **Non-pedigree Tabby Shorthair.**

Non-pedigree red-and-white shorthair

Country of origin: worldwide

Type:
shorthaired, non-pedigree

Facial characteristics:
broad round face with a short straight nose and large round eyes

Coat:
short and thick

Colors:
red-and-white

Temperament:
gentle, loving, independent, outgoing, versatile, proud

Associated breeds:
other shorthaired cats, other ginger cats

above: **Non-pedigree Red-and-White Shorthair.**

If the tabby shorthair is the most common cat there's a good chance the red-and-white shorthair comes second to it. This is an extremely robust and vigorous cat. It has faint tabby markings and is a lovely ginger color with white patches distributed at random. The red-and-white neatly avoids the problem of deafness in white cats by having some ginger and it also avoids the problem of sterility in ginger cats by having some white. And it makes sure it will survive by having the faint tabby markings. They usually have orange eyes but green is not uncommon. These are big cats with a strong muscular body. They are street-wise, pugnacious, and marvelous.

Further reading

99 Lives: Cats in History, Legend and Literature
Howard Loxton, Chronicle Books: 1998

Barron's Encyclopedia of Cat Breeds: A Complete Guide to the Domestic Cats of North America
Barron's Educational Service: 1997

The Cat and the Human Imagination: Feline Images from Bast to Garfield
Katharine M. Rogers, University of Michigan Press: 1998

Cat Breeds of the World: A Complete Illustrated Encyclopedia
Desmond Morris, Viking: 1999

The Cat Fanciers' Association Cat Encyclopedia
Will Thompson, Editor, Simon & Schuster: 1985

Cat Love: Understanding the Needs and Nature of Your Cat
Pam Johnson, Constance Oxley (Editor), Storey Books: 1990

Cat Magic: Mews, Myths, and Mystery
Patricia Telesco, Inner Traditions International Ltd.,: 1999

The Cat Name Companion: Facts and Fables to Help You Name Your Feline
Mark Bryant, Citadel Press: 1995

Cats: A Comprehensive Guide to the World's Breeds
Paddy Cutts, Thunder Bay Press: 1999

Cats in Books: A Celebration of Cat Illustration Through the Ages
Rodney Dale (Editor), Harry N Abram: 1997

Catworld: A Feline Encyclopedia
Desmond Morris, Penguin Books: 1997

The Encyclopedia of the Cat: A Unique In-depth Guide to Cat Breeds Around the World
Bruce Fogle, DK Publishing: 1997 (US); Firefly Books Ltd.: 1997 (Canada)

Identifying Cat Breeds
Paddy Cutts, BookSales Inc.: 1995

The Illustrated Encyclopedia Cat Breeds
Angela Rixon, BookSales Inc.: 1997

Legacy of the Cat: The Ultimate Illustrated Guide
Gloria Stevens, Testu Yamazaki (Photographer), Chronicle Books: 1997

The Mythology of Cats: Feline Legend and Lore Through the Ages
Gerald Hausman, Loretta Hausman, St Martins Press: 1998

The Natural Cat; Understanding Your Cat's Needs and Instincts: Everything You Should Know About Your Cat's Behavior
Helga Hofmann, Monika Wegler (Photographer), Wanda Boeke (Translator), Voyageur Press Inc: 1994

The Natural Health Cat Care Manual : An Innovative Guide to Keeping Your Cat in the Best of Health, Naturally
Don Harper, BookSales Inc.: 1994

Roger Tabor's Cat Behavior : A Complete Guide to Understanding How Your Cat Works
Roger K. Tabor, Readers Digest: 1998

The Tiger Inside: A New Approach to Caring for Your Cat
David Alderton, IDG Books Worldwide: 1998

The Tiger on Your Couch : What the Big Cats Can Teach You About Living in Harmony With Your House Cat
Bill Fleming, Quill: 1994

The Ultimate Cat Book : A Unique Photographic Guide to More Than 100 International Breeds and Varieties
David Taylor, Daphne Negus (Editor), Simon & Schuster: 1989

Wild Discovery Guide to Your Cat: Understanding and Caring for the Tiger Within
Margaret Lewis Ph.D. (Contributor), **Elizabeth Marshall Thomas** (Foreword), Discovery Book: 1999

You and Your Cat
David Taylor, Random House: 1986

Useful Addresses

American Cat Fanciers Association
P O Box 203
Point Lookout, Missouri 65726
Tel: (417) 334-5430,
Fax: (417) 334-5540
Email: info@acfacat.com
Website: *http://www.acfacat.com*
Promotes the welfare, education, knowledge, and interest in domesticated, purebred, and non-purebred cats to breeders, owners, cat exhibitors, and the public. Detailed website.

American Humane Association
63 Inverness Drive East
Englewood, Colorado 80112-5117
Tel: (303) 792-9900
Fax: (303) 792-5333
Website: *http://www.amerhumane.org*

American Society for the Prevention of Cruelty to Animals
424 East 92nd Street
New York, New York 10128-6804
Tel: (212) 876-7700
Website: *http://www.aspca.org*

Canadian Cat Association
220 Advance Blvd
Suite 101
Brampton, Ontario L6T 4J5
Tel: (905) 459-1481
Fax: (905) 459-4023
E-mail: office@cca-afc.com
Website: *http://www.cca-afc.com*
Canadian registry for purebred feline. Produces Chats Canada Cats, bilingual quarterly magazine for CCA members with show information, breeder's directory, and articles. Free to CCA members.

The Canadian Federation of Humane Societies
102-30 Concourse Gate
Nepean, Ontario K2E 7V7
Toll-Free Tel: 1-888-678-2347
Tel: (613) 224-8072
Fax: (613) 723-0252
Email: cfhs@magi.com
Website: *http://www.cfhs.ca*

Committed to ending suffering of animals. Programs, membership, publications, activities, and products.

Cat Fanciers' Almanac
P O Box 1005
Manasquan, New Jersey 08736-0805
Tel: (732) 528-9797
Fax: (732) 528-7391
E-mail: cfa@cfainc.org
Website: *http://www.cfainc.org*
Monthly publication of The Cat Fanciers' Association.

The Cat Fanciers' Association, Inc.
P O Box 1005
Manasquan, New Jersey 08736-0805
Tel: (732) 528-9797
Fax: (732) 528-7391
E-mail: cfa@cfainc.org
Website: *http://www.cfainc.org*
Worldwide registry of pedigreed cats plus cat shows, breed standards and cat care. Comprehensive website.

Cat Fancy magazine
P O Box 6050
Mission Viejo, California, 92690
Tel: (949) 855-8822
Fax: (949) 855-3045
E-mail: catfancy@fancypubs.com
Website: *http://www.catfancy.com*
On-line and print editions.

Cats magazine
P O Box 1790
Peoria, Illinois 61656
Tel Toll-Free: 1-800-829-9125
Tel: (309) 682-6626
Fax: (309) 679-5454
E-mail: info@catsmag.com
Website: *http://www.catsmag.com*
On-line and print editions.

Cats and Kittens magazine
7-L Dundas Circle
Greensboro, NC 27407-1645
Tel Toll-Free: 1-800-795-8289
Tel: (336) 292-4047
Fax: (336) 292-4272
E-mail: petbus@nr.infi.net
Website: *http://www.catsandkittens.com*

Bi-monthly publication of on-line and print editions.

CATsumer Report magazine
P O Box 10069
Austin, Texas 78766-1069
Tel Toll-Free 1-800-968-1738
Tel: (512) 454-6090
Fax: (512) 454-3420
Health, nutrition and product testing reports for cat owners.

I Love Cats magazine
450 7th Avenue
Suite 1701
New York, New York 10123-0101
Tel: (212) 244-2351
Fax: (212) 244-2387

The International Cat Association
P O Box 2684
Harlingen, Texas 78551
Tel: (956) 428-8046
Fax: (956) 428-8047
E-mail: ticaeo@xanadu2.net
Website: *http://www.tica.org*
Member-governed genetic registry of cats, including household pets. Committed to responsible breeding, advancing feline health and welfare, and fostering new breeds and colors.

Pets Magazine
505 Consumers Road.
Suite 500
Toronto, Ontario M2J 4V8
Tel Toll-Free: 1-877- 738-7624
Fax (416) 491-3996
E-mail: pets@moorshead.com
Website: *http://www.moorshead.com/pets*
Cats, dogs and other pets. On-line and print editions.

Petfinder
1273 Millstone River Road
Somerville, New Jersey 08876
Tel: (908) 904-9786
E-mail: pets@petfinder.org
Website: *http://www.petfinder.org*
On-line, searchable database of animals that need homes, plus directory of animal shelters and adoption organizations across the United States.

Index

Picture Credits

Picture Credits t – top; b – bottom; l – left; r – right; c – center

Abby Aldridge Rockefeller Folk Art Center, pages 92, 98(b), 104(t), 104(b), 105(t), 105(b), 106

Advertising Archive, page 48(br)

AKG London, pages 59 (c, Erich Lessing), 64(br), 81

Alan Robinson, pages 128, 130(l), 131, 138(t), 139(b)

Apex Photo Agency Limited, page 80(l)

Bridgeman Art Library, pages 57, 69(r)

By Permission of The British Library (with British Library shelf mark or manuscript number following in parentheses), pages 58(l); (BL 12807.3.35), 58(r); (BL C.11.c.17), 83(t); (BL C.27.a.8), 96(b); (BL 520.b.10), 97; (BL 1008459), 107; (BL 1000252), 109 (all images); (BL C.116.e.22), 112(l); (BL 12837.b.26), 114(tr); (BL 444.I.4), 115(t); (BL 12805.n.30), 117(tl) and 117(tc); (BL 012806.ee.8)

Musée D'Aquitaine de Bordeaux (Photographer– Jean-Michel Arnaud), page 41(t)

Discover Islington, pages 45(t), 117(r)

E. T. Archive, pages 12(l), 17(b), 34, 36(t), 39, 43(t), 53, 56(t), 62(t), 99, 100, 101(t), 101(b), 103, 112(r)

Faber & Faber Limited, page 108(tl)

Frederick Warne & Co, page 113(b) Illustration from ORLANDO THE MARMALADE CAT: A TRIP ABROAD by Kathleen Hale. Copyright © Kathleen Hale, 1939, 1998. Reproduced by kind permission of Frederick Warne & Co., 113(t) Illustration from THE TALE OF TOM KITTEN by Beatrix Potter. Copyright © Frederick Warne & Co., 1907, 1987. Reproduced by kind permission of Frederick Warne & Co.

Gary Roma, pages 110(t), 110(bl), 110(br), 111(tl), 111(cl), 111(bl), 111(tr), 111(br)

Haslemere Educational Museum, pages 40(tl), 40(bl)

His Grace, the Duke of Buccleuch, from his collection at Boughton House, Northamptonshire, page 98(t)

Hulton Getty Picture Collection, pages 6(b), 7(b), 37, 42(b), 43(r), 44, 45(b), 48(tr), 54(tr), 54(b), 55(b), 59(b), 60(b), 62(b), 65, 67, 68(t), 70(t), 76, 77(b), 78, 82, 83(b), 84, 86, 87, 88(t), 96(t), 116, 120, 123(t), 124

Jane Burton, pages 12(r), 13, 14(tr), 14(bl), 14(br), 15(b), 17(t), 20, 23, 27, 28, 29(t), 29(b), 31(b), 32(t), 33, 46(r), 48(bl), 50, 54(tl), 55(t), 61(t), 63(r), 68(c), 70(b), 71(b), 72, 74(l), 74(r), 77(t), 79, 81(b), 88(b), 118, 121(b), 126(b), 130(r), 138(bl), 138(br), 139(tl), 139(tr), 140, 215, 217

Kaja Vielleux, page 102(b)

Kim Taylor, pages 14(tl), 26, 32(b), 52, 85

Life File, pages 10(t), 11(l), 11(r)

Marc Henrie, Asc., pages 70(t), 183, 216

Michael Downey, page 89

Michael Le Poer French, pages 108(t), 108(b)

Ministry of Cuture, Greece, page 94(b)

National Art Museums of Sweden, page 66

Patrick Cone Photography, pages 24, 25, 30, 63(l), 121(t), 123(b), 125(l)

Petrie Museum, London University, pages 38, 61(b), 95(tl), 95(tc), 95(tr), 95(l)

Roger Tabor, pages 8, 10(b), 15(t), 18, 36(b), 40(tr), 40(br), 41(br), 42(t), 46(tl), 46(bl), 55(c), 56(b), 59(tl), 64(bl), 69(l)

Sonia Halliday Photographs, page 94(t)

Superstock Limited, jacket front cover

Tony Jedrej, pages 29(c), 47, 57, 102(t), 122(t), 127

Trinity College, University of Dublin, pages 75(t), 75(b), 95(bl), 95(br)

Witches Museum, Boscastle, page 80(t)

Ypres Tourist Information, Belgium, pages 90(t), 90(b), 91(t), 91(bl), 91(br)

Every effort has been made to ensure this listing is correct; the publisher apologizes for any omissions.